YOUR
RIGHT
TO KNOW

Sri Darwin Gross

YOUR RIGHT TO KNOW

Printed in U.S.A.
10th Printing—1981

Compiled by
Bernadine Burlin
Assisted by
Gloria Ginn

Cover Photo by an ECKist
Ink Sketches by Helen Baird
People Photo by David Court

IWP **PUBLISHING**
P.O. Box 2449
Menlo Park, CA 94025

INTRODUCTION

Heaven is right here now!!

And it is YOUR RIGHT TO KNOW how to attain the spiritual know-how that can show you the shortest, straightest route to heaven's doorway.

In a straight-forward, common sense approach rarely found in a spiritual leader, Sri Darwin Gross, the Living ECK Master of ECKANKAR, shares simple, honest truths long kept back from the masses by the controlling arm of the priestcraft, the media, the political arena, the influential.

YOUR RIGHT TO KNOW is a compilation of articles Sri Darwin Gross has written in the intervening years from October 1971 to the present time. Through the publication vehicles of the *ECK World News, The Mystic World, The ECK MATA Journal,* press releases and lecture tapes, he has extracted material that is ageless, timeless, and controversial, daring to share truths with the world consciousness of today, truths that have been kept under wraps as a control factor.

ECKANKAR, A Way of Life, was brought to the waiting world by Sri Paul Twitchell, in 1965. Twitchell has contributed over 30 books and many discourse series for home study, continuing the teachings of the ECK Masters of the Vairagi Order, begun on a master-to-chela relationship long before the records of history were chronicled.

In 1971, Sri Paul Twitchell translated (died) and Sri Darwin Gross was chosen by the ECK Masters to bring the message of the Light and Sound to the world. Writer, lecturer, spiritual guide to millions, Sri Darwin gives of himself unstintingly so that all who have the eyes to see and those who have the ears to hear can partake of truths available throughout eternity, truths that are never hidden if one hungers to return to the Godhead in this lifetime, ending the wheels of reincarnation once and for all.

It is YOUR RIGHT TO KNOW that heaven is right here now!

Bernadine Burlin

TABLE OF CONTENTS

Darwin at the ECKANKAR 7th International Youth Conference, April 16-18, 1976, Las Vegas, NV. Wherever he appears, young and old alike gather to be in his presence. —bb

Chapter 1

THE TEACHINGS OF THE VAIRAGI ECK MASTERS

In offering the spiritual teachings of the ECK Masters, as the Living ECK Master of the time, I have indeed been very fortunate in my association with them throughout this lifetime. As with Sri Paul Twitchell, the assistance was always there for they do work with the Living ECK Master of the time. There are others down through time that have had access to this teaching of ECK, who taught it, and a few who tried to write about it. To see the actual functions and workings of the law of Spirit (ECK) demonstrated by these superhuman beings and learning from them how to teach it, has been a very great honor for me. One who takes the time to live the life of ECK and learns to do the work of the Vairagi ECK Masters is entitled to respect the same as a Master in ECKANKAR.

The world is ready for this teaching in ECKANKAR for there are great numbers of individuals in every country around the world just waiting to hear the message of ECK. I would not need to write one word, for Sri Paul Twitchell presented all that is necessary for one to reach the top of the mountain, meaning experiencing the God-conscious state here and now, without waiting to die as man thinks of death.

The ECK Masters recognize all great teachers of the past as in Buddha's time. He represented the way of enlightenment, and in Jesus' day, the Christ-consciousness for which so many are seeking and are unable to completely experience until they set forth

1

on the path of ECK, as I had to.

The great spiritual awakening taking place today and over the past ten years is not due to evangelists like Billy Graham or Oral Roberts. It is due to the ECK Masters. It seems there is so much being printed today regarding the spiritual works, yet it is the same thing being repeated over and over, going back two to three thousand years of history. Man must learn to leave the past in the past and live *now* by the spiritual laws of the ECK Masters and the teachings of ECK, which is Spirit.

ECKANKAR is not a new cult, but the oldest religious teaching in all the world. The history of the ECK Masters is discussed in *The Spiritual Notebook* by Sri Paul Twitchell. I too, as some of you, have had to prove some of this for myself but some of the ECK Masters are still living in their same bodies today. Their mission: they chose to remain here on this planet of earth to assist with those Souls that are brought forth for experience in their spiritual life to reach the God-conscious state. Remember, you do not have to go off to some foreign country, climb some great mountain, such as India or Tibet, nor anywhere else, to find these great teachers. This simplicity of going to the temple within is all that is necessary.

As one enters the teachings of ECK, you should first remember not to get upset with what you read or if you do not understand a paragraph or sentence, go on. Don't sit there and let the mind haggle over it. There should be no explanations demanded of the Living ECK Master, including those ECK Masters working from the seven Golden Wisdom Temples. Until you have had a chance to go into the works of ECK thoroughly, read a couple of books, then take the lessons which come with the membership.

I've been fortunate to live and observe the daily

lives of the ECK Masters. You will find, as I have, that they at no time will influence your judgment in any way, unless it affects them directly. Then at times they will not interfere with your thoughts. Through having your experience, the ECK Masters wish you to become thoroughly convinced before one can go out into the world to give credit for the work they do and the work you will do as you unfold spiritually. You'll find there is no middle ground here; you either accept or reject what you have seen, learned, and read of this teaching of ECK.

In my trip to India, in the year of 1977, while walking along a street in Srinagar in Kashmir where I was staying, my attention was attracted to a crowd. What I saw, which was the center of interest, was one of the street magicians or fakers that are so common in that part of the world. What was being used here was hypnosis which is only a shadow of the consciousness. It has caused a great deal of comment, and those using it, and those commenting upon it, have not reached the true meaning, for there is a truth underneath it all.

One of the things that fascinated me most about the ECK Masters was, they were able to communicate with each other quicker than by thought, or as it is called, a force much more subtle than either the telephone or thought. It is known as Soul.

The following pictures are a few of the ECK Masters, of which there are many. The student who is sincere in spiritual unfoldment meets with these great beings and comes to know them through the spiritual exercises of ECK as well as in the dream state, for upon meeting any one of the ECK Masters, knowledge is imparted that can not be put into print.

FUBBI QUANTZ

ECK MASTER FUBBI QUANTZ

Fubbi Quantz is the head of the Katsupari Monastery in the Thanglha Mountains of northern Tibet, and guardian of the first section of the holy book of ECKANKAR, The Shariyat-Ki-Sugmad (Way of the Eternal).

Said to have had 19 teachers so as to gain his place in the universe, Fubbi Quantz served as Living ECK Master during the time of Buddha in India. He immortalized his body and became the Abbot of the Katsupari Monastery, the Temple of Golden Wisdom on the Surati Lok, known as the mountain world, where the Ayur Vedha, a system of rejuvenation is followed.

GOPAL DAS

ECK MASTER GOPAL DAS

Gopal Das was the Living ECK Master around 3,000 B.C., during the time of Ramses II, when the Pyramids were being built by the Pharaohs at Sakkara in Egypt.

Much of the base-twelve number system in early use during the ancient Egyptian times was due to the efforts of Gopal Das. He introduced a simple system which was considered the duo-decimal system which is the reckoning by 12 in common use today. The priestcraft tried to withhold it from the public, but he was able to give out enough information, especially among the ECK disciples of his time, and gradually in the centuries that followed the system became better known and found favor in public education. He was also responsible for introducing licorice into Egypt for medical purposes.

A rather tall, thin man with light golden hair and a full face, his eyes light blue, he teaches and acts as guardian of the holy book, The Shariyat-Ki-Sugmad, at the Askleposis Temple of Golden Wisdom in the city of Sahasra-dal-Kanwal on the Anda Lok, known as the astral world.

LAI TSI

ECK MASTER LAI TSI

This great Chinese ECK Master is the guardian of The Shariyat-Ki-Sugmad at the Temple of Golden Wisdom in the city of Arhirit located on the Saguna Lok, known as the etheric world.

Tiny in stature, Lai Tsi wears a Chinese hat, has a small goatee and a thin, wrinkled face with sunken dark eyes, and a warm smile. He wears an embroidered robe of dark maroon.

Born into a family of great wealth, Lai Tsi received his higher education from one of the great monastic universities in Tibet. He retired to a cave, befriending the wild animals, concluding that realization could only be found in stillness and solitude of nature. However, he was visited daily by the ECK Master Yaubl Sacabi, learning the liberation of Soul through the teachings of ECKANKAR, and returned to the world to fulfill his responsibility as Living ECK Master of the times.

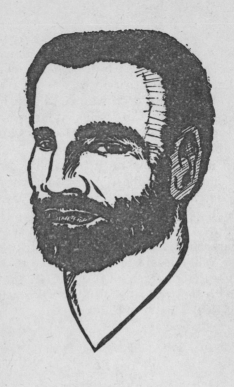

REBAZAR TARZS

ECK MASTER REBAZAR TARZS

Rebazar Tarzs was born in the year 1461, in the mountain village of Sarana in northern Tibet. He looks to be in his middle thirties but is thought to be over 500 years old in his physical body. Black hair closely cropped to his head, coal-black eyes that pierce the heart, a neatly trimmed black beard, he carries his 6-foot frame, 185 pounds majestically, his maroon robe and wooden staff a familiar sight in the spiritual city of Agam Des where he teaches at the famous ECK-Marg School of Wisdom.

He developed into mastership under the spiritual guidance of Yaubl Sacabi. It was Rebazar Tarzs who was responsible for the inner guidance of Christopher Columbus. Rebazar stayed on earth for 75 years teaching ECK, then he retired in the same body to the mountain vastness of the Hindu Kush Mountains of the Himalayas. He has spiritually developed several ECK Masters, and is responsible for passing the Rod of ECK Power from one Master to his successor. He is known as the Torchbearer of ECKANKAR.

PEDDAR ZASKQ

ECK MASTER PEDDAR ZASKQ

A quiet Southern gentleman, born along the Mississippi River, Peddar Zaskq (Sri Paul Twitchell) brought the modern-day teachings of ECKANKAR to the world through his books, writings, tapes, lectures and travels. He served as a gunnery officer in the United States Navy during World War II. After extensive training by Rebazar Tarzs, the Torchbearer of ECKANKAR, Paul accepted the spiritual mantle of MAHANTA, Living ECK Master, from 1965 until his translation (death) in 1971.

Under the tutelage of Rebazar Tarzs, Paul brought spiritual experiences never before understood to the waiting world with such controversial books as *The Tiger's Fang, The Flute of God;* beautiful books of love and excitement in *Stranger by The River, The Way of Dharma* and *Drums of ECK. Dialogues With The Master* contained discourses between the ECK Master Rebazar Tarzs and his chela, Paul Twitchell.

Paul trained his successor, Sri Darwin Gross (Dap Ren), who accepted the spiritual mantle of MAHANTA, Living ECK Master, following Paul's translation in September 1971.

Chapter 2

THE GOLDEN PRECEPTS OF ECKANKAR

The Golden Precepts of ECKANKAR and its teachings of ECK are about what the mystics of all religions have referred to as The Way or The Path. In ECKANKAR it is the middle path and is The Dharma, The Way, the journey of the pilgrim Soul towards and into the heart of the SUGMAD, or God. One discovers Self and eventually all must travel this pathway. Some find it stumbly, seemingly by hap or hazard. Many do not know that there is The Way called ECK, still less that there is a guide to direct their spiritual steps. For the few only is there a certain knowledge of this, yet in the end, both for the few and the many, the Living ECK Master is the spiritual guide for those who are bold enough to step on the Path of ECK. He teaches on a one-to-one basis when the individual reaches the Soul Plane, then is turned loose and must proceed on his own individually in his spiritual unfoldment.

The teachings of ECK are universal and whatever bears the stamp of universality is rooted in truth. Truth cannot be understood by all men, for the beginner as well as for the esoteric student, for the occidental as well as for the oriental, ECKANKAR and its teachings of ECK have something to offer each. Wherever one stands in life the first steps to obtain it can be taken because truth is never denied any man if in his heart he asks for it. He will be led to the temple within which is far greater than any temple man can build.

The goal of the chela in ECK is the God-enlightened state which comes by the practice of

ECKANKAR and its spiritual exercises, the secret science of total awareness. It is always an overwhelming experience to the chela. It is also found when the chela shares such an experience with others, the shock is often too much for their less sensitive states of consciousness.

I would like to point out here that ECK is the mainstream of Life out of which all doctrines flow. It is the basic teachings of religious belief, philosophy and other doctrines on the fulfillment of life. Due to this hidden factor in the nature of the SUGMAD (God), the revelation of ECK will be a shock when it strikes the individual. It upsets one's faith in cherished beliefs. Man is conditioned by opinions and authorities, about human thinking. It is not the goal of those in ECK nor the movement of ECKANKAR to upset the individual in his particular faith nor to pull them off their path as many other religions try to do. This is breaking a spiritual law of God.

In ECKANKAR one learns at his early stage that there are three basic cardinal principles, which means the three laws of the SUGMAD.

(1) The first law which consists of the Master, the Bani, or the Sound Current, and Jivan Mukti, the spiritual freedom.

(2) The second law which consists of Self-Realization or Self-knowledge, God-Realization or God-knowledge, and entering into the kingdom of heaven, either in this life or the next.

(3) The third law which consists of the Darshan, meeting with the Master and being recognized by him, the divisions of the spiritual and material worlds, and the Atma Sarup, known as the Soul body.

The Darshan can be experienced in your spiritual contemplative exercises in ECKANKAR. There are many and one must find that spiritual exercise that suits him for the vibratory rate of each individual varies greatly. One of these exercises that appears in the ECK books or ECK discourses will work for the individual and start to unfold him and give him some experience. That which he has gotten ahold of here, it is greater than any of man's inventions.

Meeting the Master and being recognized by him, known as the Darshan, does not have to take place in the physical. It can take place in the dream state, or as I have mentioned, in the spiritual contemplative exercises. For some the Master will appear to the individual in the bedroom, at their place of work or out in the woods or playing on the playground. It matters not where the individual is, what he does to make his way in this world, but that he becomes responsible and recognizes his responsibilities. There are steps leading up to the Darshan which the individual chela, an Initiate on the Path of ECK, must recognize and prepare or develop himself spiritually for the next step.

Once the individual in ECK understands the Precepts of ECKANKAR, he no longer seeks for he becomes a Spiritual Traveler on the Path of ECK. He sees that mind is *not* power. This revelation shocks anyone steeped in the teaching that right thinking can resolve all of his physical problems or spiritual problems. The Living ECK Master's role is to lead the chela out of darkness into the divine light of the highest kingdom. Thus he will gain spiritual freedom, and knowledge will be the greatest of all wisdoms, not gained from stories or books but from contact with God Itself.

The individual in ECKANKAR is not brainwashed for ECKANKAR and its teachings are not a cult or sect in any way, as many of those who have taken a look at its teachings or without investigating it properly have come to believe that it is just another religion.

There is no tithing as in other religions, and some religions demand a certain portion of the individual's money and determine what it should be according to how much that individual makes. And this is basically true with most religions. Others practice austerities. In ECKANKAR there are no austerities. It is and always will be an individual path, the individual chooses himself whether or not he wishes to take the next step. They are not forced in any direction.

For those that work in the ECKANKAR International Office or take some area of responsibility, must have and do have greater ethics, otherwise they find themselves in turmoil. The laws of karma will come into play very swiftly. The chela in ECK has the linkup in initiation and it takes the Living ECK Master to do that, but the Word, or that which we know as the Sound Current is the reactivation within himself to establish himself again in the kingdom of heaven. In other words, initiation is simply that which gets him to have self-recognition. This is why it has been stressed that one must take a little initiative, he is not forced or told that he must do this or that. It is up to the individual every step of the way. His goal should be that of Self-Realization first, and then God-Realization, and third, to be a co-worker with God during this lifetime, here and now.

I am asked many times, "I want to be a co-worker, what do you want me to do, Darwin? How can I be a co-worker?" My answer to that individual is, whatever he desires in his life, in his spiritual life that he's going to do, is what he is going to do in his mission with God. If he's going to be a healer, that is part of his mission in this world. If he's going to be

17

something else of this nature, then this is part of his mission. One must remember that basically he becomes a channel like the Master, he becomes a channel through which the Living ECK Master can work, and let the ECK power flow through and reach out to those who the ECK Master cannot reach because of lack of sympathy for the works of ECKANKAR, but a sympathy between the chela and this individual who might resist the ECK Master but wouldn't resist the chela.

Now all of this might seem a little odd, a little foreign to the person to say that by becoming a chela of ECK I'm giving up my life, I'm giving up everything in life to do this. This is not quite true because what we're doing here actually within this work of ECK is trying to get the chela to accept the will of God. The chela in order to accept the will of God must give up his inner life to the ECK Master, not the physical Master, but the Inner Master in his radiant form and let the Inner Master take over and direct his life because it will be through him that God will work to give the directions and to carry him and take him into the higher life. Then when he begins to move into the pure positive God Worlds in the higher life, eventually he will not need this anymore, and he is directly taken and given all the work and knows his mission and carries out his duties and he can follow directly from the Lord to him. Then eventually he becomes the Master himself.

One keeps in mind that the Master is only an instrument and because he is the instrument he himself has no will, in a sense, of his own. He has a will like anyone else normally does but he must think in the terms that whatever God gives him to do he is going to follow out and do this. It doesn't mean he doesn't know the meaning between yes and no and right from wrong and all of these factors that we have to go through daily. But he is given the direction by the Lord through the vehicle which is the ECK Master, and the Master doesn't say no. He doesn't say "now do this" or "you do that," but the power, the ECK ITSELF (and ECK is Spirit or that which some religious teachings call the Holy Ghost, it's one and the same) is flowing through the Master, reaches out and IT of ITSELF takes and directs and moves the individual within a certain direction and all of this means then that there's no word vocally or written that does this.

An individual that is guided and listens to the Master will have far greater ethics than man knows. As one expands his consciousness and is developed spiritually, as Sri Paul Twitchell pointed out in *The Spiritual Notebook*, their moral characteristics far exceed that which man also knows and beyond what is practiced by the various religions or philosophical teachings today.

Chapter 3

THE WORD OF GOD

When there are no harsh words of another man, animal or thing, the love of SUGMAD (God) is realized in silence and in secrecy, evidences itself in deeds of loving kindness. In the MAHANTA's Love there is no criticism, no judgment and no condemnation.

There have been many spiritual teachers of the past who have told us that one should not look to just food of the earth to live by but to seek out the Word through the Sound Current that issues out of the SUGMAD. The experiences of those who have listened are many by both men and women, that life does not consist of just work, food and rest, but that factor of Life which is far more important, the Word of God known as Shabda, Bani.

The Shabda has been spoken of as the Living Waters of Life, the Bread of Life. This is the security of the ECKists. It is through the ECK (Spirit), the radiant form of the Living ECK Master, that they have the protection. As one goes about his tasks and duties, even though one may go through rough water, or experience of the fire, the waters will not sweep you under nor will the flames fall upon you, but around you, should the Word of God be within you and flow forth from the temple within you. It is that nectar, your bread and water of life, as the bread and fishes Jesus spoke of. The Word can be the one from your initiation or one from the God Worlds of ECK. It wants to be a vital living force within you. By allowing the ECK within your world it must become part of your consciousness. Then the

ECK can function for the good of all eternally should we keep it alive within us.

In meeting the ECKists from different parts of the world, it is always a joy for me to be with those on the Path of ECK. With my travels, regardless of what part of the world I've been to, I have found that there are two things necessary in the ECK chela's training which some individuals lack in order for them to enter into the spiritual worlds. First I will say this does not just exist overseas but in the North American continent as well. It was stated by Rebazar Tarzs that, "Nothing should move the dwellers in ECK! He must live in God and nothing else. The influence of the psychic worlds shall not touch him."

The many schools of thought and religions hardly let a person get above the psychic planes as Sri Paul Twitchell has stated many times. Naive people posing as religious leaders often lead their more naive followers into the areas of danger by not being able to give them spiritual assistance in the psychic worlds.

It amazes me that so many people want to alter their environment until they have control over it and hope to achieve happiness. This is age-old and no individual nor group of people can change the environment to suit themselves without hurting others.

A basic factor of all social ills within the world and all planes within the psychic worlds is that reformers and religions, east and west, are preaching peace on earth or anywhere in the universe. The psychic worlds are ruled by the dark force, Kal, which will never allow it to happen, for Kal is under the direction of the Great One called SUGMAD (God).

With the above being true, what is necessary first in the ECK Initiate's training is that when we are the result of an outward or overt behaviour due to our thoughts, feelings or emotions, outbursts of these occupying space in any given situation in this material universe will affect us in a covert manner.

Most often this goes against our very nature as well as our relationships with others. This can be in the atmosphere of an office, an airport, terminal or on the street where thoughts pass through daily leaving behind mixed emotions of rage, sorrow, discouragement and various negative feelings. Most sensitive persons can pick up these emotional states without knowing it and react overtly against anyone in their line of fire.

The second part of the Initiate's training is that one must never allow their reactions to these influences to run willy-nilly. The individual must take charge of that. To have conscious awareness of the influence of some negative nature and react to it will not work. We must learn to counteract it.

Should one choose to control the environment he must start with the control of self. When one is unable to be influenced by surrounding conditions one can never hope to exercise any influence over them. As Sri Paul Twitchell pointed out that the paradox of the above statement is that "when we cease to be concerned about the environment, we will have the power to change it."

Beautiful indeed is the bond between the Living ECK Master and the chela. The common sense on the part of the Initiate of utmost confidence and love so that nothing he feels could be hid from the Living ECK Master's knowledge, and on the part of the Living ECK Master, the understanding, the compassion and the love equally divided to each Initiate. If the chela has gratitude towards the Living ECK Master, then he, in a sense, has gratitude for the Initiate, for he sees in the chela the flowering vehicle for the SUGMAD and a new master of compassion coming forth during this lifetime and not waiting for the eons to be a co-worker with God.

Your attention and the degree of concentration you give it, can influence your imagination and do that which you ask of it. In ECK and your daily life, all fulfillment of all your desires depend upon your control of concentration of your awareness, for the Kal wants you to concentrate on the "things" of this world for his benefit.

Your attention may be either attracted from without or directed from within. For most people the attention is either attracted from without when you are consciously occupied with the external impressions of the immediate surroundings. For the Higher Initiates who continue their spiritual exercises and unfold spiritually, will find that they are not moved by external impressions but follow the inner guidance of the Living ECK Master, the Inner Master. For if you stop to think about it, the very lines of this paragraph are attracting your attention. Is it from within or without? The attention of the individual is directed from within if you deliberately choose what you will be preoccupied with mentally.

It is easy to see that in the objective world that one's attention is not only attracted by, but is constantly directed to, external impressions should you let them be so directed. However, with the help of the Living ECK Master, the Inner Master, your control in the subjective world can be mastered. This is interesting. For the masses it is non-existent; this is interesting for the ECKists, for in this state, attention is usually the servant of the Kal force and not the Master as in the ECK, of your world. There is a great variation directed objectively and attention directed subjectively and the capacity to change your future depends on the latter.

When you, as a Higher Initiate, an ECKist, are able to control the movements of your attention in the subjective world, you can modify or alter your life as you wish. However, this control cannot be achieved if you allow your attention to be attracted constantly from without. For example: listen to gossip of others or be influenced by what you see the rest of the world doing. Each day set yourself the duty of deliberately withdrawing your attention from the world around you on the outer and focus it subjectively by doing a spiritual exercise, such as The Easy Way, page 90 of *In My Soul I Am Free*.

In other words, put your attention on the ECK or those thoughts you do not understand, then those things that have restricted you will fade and drop away. The day you achieve control of the movements of your attention in the subjective world, through the spiritual exercises of ECK, you become master of your own fate.

You no longer accept the dominance of the outside world and its conditions, nor its circumstances. You will then stand forth, say "I am an ECKist, I will not accept life on the basis of the external world." Once having achieved control of the movements of your attention and discovered the mystery hid from the masses, that ECK flows through you Divine, then you will accept the ECK as supremacy in all things.

Chapter 4

THE SPIRITUAL BODY OF MAN

It is all too clear that our age suffers from a vast hunger and impoverishment of the spirit of ECK which the organized religions are unable to satisfy or give succor to their people. It would be easy to blame the modern world for ignoring Christianity or Buddhism or Hinduism or Islam, etc., to condemn it as merely perverse heathenism, if church religion showed any strong signs of spiritual life. The truth, however, is that with some varied and scattered expectations, the church religions are spiritually dead. Some of the best minds of the church admit and deplore it openly.

Outside and even within the church, modern man is therefore indifferent to religion, and yet his nervous restlessness, his chronic sense of frustration, his love of sensationalism as an escape, his fitful use of every substitute for religion from snake worship to getting drunk show that his Soul still desires a release from Itself. That infusion of life in many, though being possessed by a power greater than itself, is found perfectly in union with God alone.

What IS religion or a religious organization? Religion may be defined as a bond uniting man to God. You'll find it very difficult to define religion or a religious organization. It has been attempted by many courts, encyclopedias and secondary sources. Some of the definitions might be interesting to look up. Not only might you find good ol' faith and worship, but also how one thinks. Religion includes a belief not necessarily referring to a supernatural power; it could involve an association openly

25

expressing its beliefs.

ECKANKAR teaches that there is no death, which alone constitutes a belief. There are many other beliefs similar such as a sacred relationship, a personal experience an ECKist might have with the Living ECK Master during the contemplative spiritual exercises or in the higher realms of heaven.

At this point it would be good to point out the differences between ECKANKAR and ECK. ECKANKAR, the Ancient Science of Soul Travel, is the movement of the inner consciousness which travels through the lower states until it ascends into the etheric states. Here the subject feels he possesses an awareness of the religious experience of "being." This awareness is achieved through a series of spiritual exercises known only to followers of this ancient science. This you will find is written throughout all the ECK works, not only in the physical but in the spiritual realms as well, in the Golden Wisdom Temples of ECKANKAR.

ECK, the Science of Total Awareness, grows out of the experience of Soul Travel. The subject gains the state of religious awareness at his *own* volition via the spiritual exercises of ECKANKAR. The latter is correlated only with the movement of the inner consciousness (Soul) within the regions of time and space. The ECK goes above these regions beyond time and space, for ALL is omniscient, omnipresent, omnipotent, hence the term "Total Awareness."

This total awareness is a key we use to enter the kingdom of God. It is a channel, a tunnel, or what other groups call the Christ consciousness, the Buddha consciousness, the Krishna consciousness. This state known to us as ECKshar is what we must all come to and go through to become the ECK (Spirit). We must spiritualize the mind and body by saturating ourselves with the spiritual ideal of the Living ECK Master and the ECK.

ECK must therefore come first in the life of every Initiate and IT will demand more and more of the individual until IT has all of him. The person will suffer, cry, complain and resist all changes the ECK is making within him, but it is a useless struggle and the sooner he ceases to fight against any changes, the sooner he gains true freedom.

ECK is the shortest way to God. This is our basic teaching. Whenever man pursues creeds, priests and organizations, he will find a religion of some sort, but never the way to enter the kingdom of God as stated by the great ECK Masters.

The main teaching of ECKANKAR is that if the chela faithfully practices the spiritual exercises, he will enter the kingdom of heaven while still living in the human body. This is the fundamental difference between ECK and all other religions. Also, ECK alone offers a living leader, the Living ECK Master, for as spiritual law clearly states, the chela in a human body must have a master in the human body

I find many do not understand that the knowledge of ECKANKAR is not a slow product of evolution, an accumulation of learning gathered during long ages of study. It is not the sum of knowledge accumulated in libraries to be memorized by students, nor a record or acquired information. The knowledge of the ECK known by the spiritual travelers is unique. Every traveler gains the whole sum of metaphysics anew during his travels. His knowledge of the ECK is gained by a definite line of individual endeavor and personal experience. It is not something gathered up by him from many sources but is gained from within himself by the expansion of his own consciousness.

Any man may gain this development and this

metaphysical knowledge provided he uses the scientific method of the spiritual travelers in ECK. In the light of this illuminating fact, one of the assumptions of the worldly knowledge disappears, that a definite and certain knowledge of the ECK cannot be acquired.

We find the mainspring of every civilization is its church. When that decays the civilization decays with it. But with the ECK one finds no decay for ITS strength lies in the SUGMAD (God) and therein IT is all powerful. Those who follow the ECK find that it needs no human state of consciousness to guide it as religions do. The chief commandments that run like a golden thread through the teachings of every Living ECK Master have all come from the teachings of the SUGMAD. A Living ECK Master has always been present in every civilization in history. Those Divine Ones came out in public when their help was most needed, when spirituality was its lowest ebb in some country of the world, or planet, and when materialism was apparently victorious.

Each Living ECK Master in his respective time laid down the spiritual law over and over again to help those who follow the path of ECK. These laws which are Truth have always existed to lead man to God. The priestcraft has taken the laws of ECK and made them into tenets of organized religion. Therefore, idealistically, Spirit (the ECK), in the mode of force that prevailed during each period of the Living ECK Master, has all but disappeared due to the weight of orthodox dogma.

The Living ECK Masters always have the responsibility to not establish new religious cults or mystery schools. Instead, they rejuvenate the religious thoughts of all people and instill a higher understanding of life in them. Those who have been founders of dogmatic religions have passed away leaving little. Those who seek will find the ECKANKAR teachings are completely intact in their lineage through the centuries, as I have found and learned that the science of ECK knowledge could not be taught, but rather caught. And once caught, one never has to be in physical association with the higher beings or teachings again. I also have had association with them and all teachings anywhere and everywhere in all worlds, on all planets, with all beings, regardless of where they might be. Teachings of ECK in ECKANKAR will always remain for the individual.

It is necessary to have both the Light and Sound in your spiritual life. As you know the Light is for the traveling Soul to see the pitfalls and obstructions on Its journey to God, and the Sound is for Soul to follow the path back to the throne of the King of Kings to the SUGMAD. So you must make contact with both aspects of the Word within thyself. And this is provided by God and unfolded by the true Godman, the Living ECK Master of the time, along with the Sound, step by step into the land of pure and eternal bliss.

Many of the Christian saints as well as those from the East have written about their struggles to overcome the negative force and reach God, and yet that struggle is not necessary. There is an easier path to God via the ECK.

The way to God is difficult for those who struggle against the little self and look to the obstacles in the path. The difference between Heaven and Earth as stated in *Stranger by the River,* by Sri Paul Twitchell, is hardly a hairbreadth apart.

Remember, those who talk too much about the supreme ECK and those who talk too much about realization are usually wandering around in their own minds and are in the throes of struggle. If you will think on this fact, that the ability to go beyond one's self does not come easily, then you will know that too many hope to find it as an easy path to God.

You will find not only the present Living ECK Master but the past masters will seldom ever put faith, trust or love in any man who is submerged completely in the negative current. He will not waste time or be bothered unless that Soul is actually a highly developed one lost in it. Also, he does not look back to see who's following or who's on the path. I don't have time for that.

It's interesting that the higher one is spiritually unfolded and drops off the path or steps aside, the harder it is to get back on the path after a fall from grace. One must be indifferent with that kind of person that is steeped in negativity. It's hard to make one understand the real intrinsic points of the spiritual body of man and its needs, productions and functions. It is so simple and really so very unwise of anyone to say that the Master will take care of him. THAT is a lazy man's way of saying it and it is cited often by the lazy devotees that God is taking care of him and he will give many examples, but they mean nothing. Tell me, how will God take care of anyone who is too lazy or too busy to pray or contemplate?

Chapter 5

BE GOOD TO YOURSELF SPIRITUALLY

With all the emphasis that is being brought forth on a healthy body, the awareness that is being presented to the masses about the junk foods, various chemicals, preservatives and the different types of solutions that we put into our body, all tend to clog our veins, cause various health problems. This starts while we are young and builds up as we get older. The body is under the rule of the mental realm, the mind. The mind being the computer, the body must obey, so it's the information that we obtain, whether it's via television or the books we read and that which we hear. The mind must choose or automatically express when certain thoughts are allowed to send forth these signals from the mind to various parts of the body, and with unlawful thoughts, the body sinks rapidly into fatigue or disease and sometimes decay. On the other side of the coin when the commands of happy thoughts, beautiful thoughts and glad tidings are sent forth, it becomes as a youth out in the field on a spring day.

The individual must recognize that one's health, circumstances, are rooted deeply in thought. Should you have sickly thoughts, it will be expressed and manifest into the body. The teachings of ECK stress that thoughts of fear can be eliminated but it stems from getting to know yourself for there are many stories daily in the newspapers and magazines about how fear killed some man or some woman. Let the Living ECK Master help you over this obstacle. Fear is continually disabling life here in the physical realm by the thousands every year. Those individuals

31

who live in fear of disease or sickness usually are the people who receive it. As the Living ECK Master I bear some of this for some; however, do not feel sorry for I do not have to do this. Anxiety is one of the Kal traps that an individual must watch for, for it lays open the entrance to the body, with disease, very quickly via the mind. Negative thoughts and impure thoughts are a real hazard to the nervous system. If you are the type of individual that receives a negative thought occasionally, stamp it out with placing your attention either on the ECK or the Inner Master. Or if you don't look to either, place your attention on God, if that's possible, and you'll find that you'll overcome these negative thoughts. They'll start to be fewer. Strong and happy thoughts build up the body to withstand the strain of the day as well as having it healthy and beautiful. Your body is a very delicate and plastic instrument which responds rapidly to the thoughts with which it is impressed, and your habits of thought will produce their effects, good or bad, upon it.

Herbs, The Magic Healers by Sri Paul Twitchell certainly can guide the individual to a healthier diet in order to build a strong body. Not only strong but healthy, for health and feeling good allows one to develop spiritually to his fullest, but the individual must determine for himself what makes him feel good by the things he drinks and eats. As Jesus put it: "Take no thought of what you eat or drink," but when you look in the mirror and find that you don't look healthy and you've outgrown your shirt, you must do something about that yourself.

Sri Paul Twitchell in *Herbs, The Magic Healers* tells us: "Oftentimes when people are burdened with negative emotions niacin and Vitamin B nutrients will resolve the sour attitude. It is known among health authorities that illnesses of this nature can result when either environmental factors or chemicals produced in the body upset the ratio of various molecules carried by the blood to the brain. Any deficiency of nutrients needed to nourish the brain can also cause an imbalance in the body and brain."

The importance of enzymes, their abilities to digest food, rebuild prepared foods into muscle, nerve, bone or glands, eliminate poisons in the system, assist longevity, coagulate and stop bleeding, are detailed in this book.

Herbs have long been a part of our history. Alexander the Great distributed licorice root among his own troops for medical purposes just as a modern soldier carries his own first aid supply in campaigns. The Roman Legionnaires also considered licorice an indispensable ration for their grueling campaigns on the Roman frontiers. The Buddhists later adopted it as a sacred symbol for their ceremonies and rituals.

Many historical characters have been greatly addicted to sweets: Hitler, Napoleon, Queen Elizabeth I, Alexander the Great, Stalin, Julius Caesar, Queen Victoria. They may have subjected themselves to the metabolic paradox of creating a condition of low blood sugar by eating too much sugar. Adolf Hitler was the most famous vegetarian of our times. In order to compensate for the lack of zest in his diet, which was likely due to lack of meat protein, he went to extremes with sweets. Denmark which has the highest suicide rate in the world has an average yearly intake of 124 pounds of sugar per person.

A mineral rich person is a happy one and often very successful in his work. He radiates a personality so different and unusual that he is often admired instantly upon meeting him. So many minerals of various types are needed by the body to provide health and enjoyment of life and they should never be overlooked.

I get a good number of letters from individuals that are asking for help. They have eaten an enormous amount of what are known as Kal foods for twenty, thirty or forty years, and all of a sudden their joints are stiffened up. They have eaten a lot of sugar, chemically treated sugar, a lot of chemically treated salt, and other chemicals. I know of one individual that took the rice diet; she was about forty-five years old and had been laid up with arthritis for more than twenty years. After the ten-day rice diet (this is brown rice not white rice), she was able to run up her stairs and move her fingers where she had not been able to walk up the stairs in the last ten years. But she had the faith of being healed, having enormous amount of the foreign chemicals removed from her bloodstream.

However, if you do go on the rice diet, especially an older person, go easy with it, eat a few vegetables, fresh vegetables, and maybe salad or something along with it. Myself, when I first went on it to find out what the results would be, I went at it slow. I took more than ten days; the results were terrific. Usually a younger person is not bothered by the chemicals and does not have to clean out the blood until the years add up. However, today the youth are very health conscious and are aware of what they eat.

There are other methods. The early men or those from the old country, what is known as Europe, had used wheat, a grain, or barley for the same purposes, going on a fast of just grain, no meats or other foods other than perhaps some fresh vegetables—this be it a whole wheat or barley can have the same effect as brown rice. I will not go into which one came about first by man, but both of them have been used a great length of time.

Without nourishment for the body, spiritual or physical, no life is impossible. To eat in some form, whether it is like those particular ECK Masters of the Ancient Order of the Vairagis, the God Eaters, who partake of the ECK life force, or the man on the material level with two full meals a day, is to create new life for tomorrow through the sacrifice of the lower realms, including the herbal kingdom. It was learned long ago that the body structure changes by eating, that the nature of man can be changed by the manner in which he eats and drinks.

Through Spirit in the teachings of ECK, one learns that to receive more we must give of what we have received. This is passing on to others information whether it's on health or spiritual growth and how to obtain it, by letting others should they ask, know, whether you write or talk to the individual.

If we withhold what we receive, stagnation sets in and we'll be like the wheel that generates power from the water and suddenly of its own volition begins to withhold the water it is using. What happens is that it soon finds itself stifled with inert water. It is only when the water is allowed to flow freely through that it is of value to the wheel to create the power, and that is true of man as well. Spirit must freely be allowed to flow through us individually. When one connects through the initiations in ECKANKAR with Spirit, ideas flow. If spiritual knowledge is gained then this must be given out a little at a time to others in some manner in order to receive the benefit from what you have received and to gain more. One must allow others to do the same that they may grow and develop as he is growing.

As one learns spiritually how to let Spirit flow

through and be a vehicle for God, you'll find the Inner Master working with you, not only trying to assist in overcoming negative habits or negative thoughts, and even those negative thoughts that are impressed upon the body that make the body ill.

Health and happiness means to be rid of fatigue and disease. To have a good appetite, good memory, good humor and precision in thought and action, to be free from anxiety and fear, to have a great capacity for survival over illness and anxieties, to have joy, long life and great spiritual adventures.

Chapter 6

ABORTION: THE WOMAN'S RIGHT

The religious orders are attempting to convince not only all women, but the Government as well, that the unborn child is a person. This is not so. The fetus is a biological entity only. The whole point is that Soul, which is that individual spark of God, does not enter the body while it is in the womb of the female, but only *after* the child has been brought into the outer world, and sometimes later than that.

Therefore, it is not murder if the woman decides not to bear the child and carry the responsibilities of feeding it, seeing it through school and out into life, any more than it is murder if I cut off a bit of skin from my finger. It is her decision alone; there is no Karma attached. There is nothing but the guilt and fear that has been pressed upon her through man's ignorance.

In the East, India for example, there exists worship of a feminine principle that is referred to as the Kali, the mother goddess. Kali is the consort of Shiva, one of the Hindu Trinity who is the offspring of Brahm, ruler of the mental world. ECKists know Brahm as Kal, or Kal Niranjan, the negative force, but many religions mistakenly worship him as the Supreme Lord.

Brahm, according to Hindu tradition, married Shakti and had three sons, which in the Hindu mind are personifications of the three currents which exist in these lower worlds: Brahma, the creator; Vishnu, the preserver; and Shiva, the destroyer. Kali, the mother principle, who married Shiva, is the goddess of destruction. She destroys all, yet replaces it with the fertility of life. In other words, she is a sex goddess. She represents the great womb of the universe and out of her womb is born all life. The Hindus look upon all life as the feminine principle, because they are taught that womanhood is greater than manhood.

India's religious system spread far West and East during its advent. Though there are not many powerful Hindu cults established in the West, the influence of Hinduism has been so strong that it replaced sections of thought in China and Japan, and to the West, in most of the nations along the Mediterranean coast.

Christianity adopted the Virgin Mother idea from the Indian philosophy (mainly Shakti, Mother of the triad group) and completely lifted it and fashioned it into a westernized idea. The whole point is that Kali has become the symbol of the feminine mind. The whole mystery of the feminine principle is found in the Kali symbol.

Priestcraft taught man long ago that motherhood was greatest because out of it comes the birth of all life. Yet beyond this thought can be seen that Maya, illusion, is the veil through which life comes. Soul steps across from the higher planes through the veil of Maya to incarnate in the body of the child after it is born, animating it beyond mere biological existence.

Now the word Maya has a dozen meanings. In the West it can be seen as Marie, Mary, May, Molly, Polly, etc. Hence comes the Mary who gave birth to the savior Jesus, yet he only used her body in order to visit this planet.

Western psychology puts an undue emphasis upon an aberration of its men: that man longs to return to the womb for its comfort, where he slept in soft darkness, protected by the woman's belly, and fed without struggle. This emphasis creates the symbol in man's mind that the unborn child is a person, and his fear and guilt in the matter of abortion.

It is primarily men who advocate the legislation against legalized abortion, and this is a reflection of both the worship of the feminine principle, and a perversion of it which causes men to attempt to hold women down by imprisoning them within this role against their will. Even in the Roman Catholic faith, officially radically opposed to abortion, women are known to be far more liberal about abortion than the rigidly indoctrinated men, and often seek abortions in secrecy.

If the female population becomes aware of the oppression, discrimination and injustice the anti-abortion movement represents, there could be massive uprisings by the women of all nations. Man is trying to put down the choice of the individual woman to decide for herself whether or not she wants the responsibility throughout the rest of her physical life of bringing a child into the physical world.

For the woman in ECKANKAR, it is simply her choice. There is no guilt factor for the ECKists, because they have the understanding to know that life is not limited to just this plane of awareness and that there is no death as man thinks of it.

Each of us as individuals choose and control our lives and it is not someone else's part either through religion or legislation to attempt to dictate the good of all mankind.

A great deal more on this subject may be found in the book *The Far Country* by Sri Paul Twitchell.

Chapter 7

CHILDREN IN ECK

The children in ECK fit a very important role in the ECK society. These children are an expression of the ECK and it is of a very spiritual nature for two people who are deeply in love, for the woman to bear the husband a child. The responsibility these two people have for their children is seeing they have a home to grow up in, to feed and clothe them, and in today's world, discipline and educate them so they can make their way in life. The responsibility of spiritual growth and development that the ECK parent has is one which many do not recognize nor understand, let alone uphold. Through spiritual training and the teachings of ECK at a very early age, a foundation is being built for that child that is greater than any other teaching on this planet.

The ethics of these children will be higher than any other group, and most young people studying ECK will find their grades, if poor, will improve. They will straighten out in many areas. Emotions should not be suppressed nor should the child be taught to suppress them. There are no bad or good emotions, they are only emotions. By "controlling" the emotions, if started at an early age, an individual becomes much stronger than the average citizen, for years are added onto his life. This is the secret of longevity.

The children of today who are studying ECK are, and will be, the backbone of the ECKANKAR movement tomorrow. Children should be allowed to go along at their own speed; do not push, it's best to encourage but not to push. If the parent is reading or discussing ECK with children and they become disinterested, then stop where you are and pick up later. Let them grow at their own pace. Children will have varied experiences, different from their ECK parents, or from other children's, so no comparisons should be made. Let them experience in their own way.

The parents can help their children take the first step onto the Path by teaching them the principles of ECK and help them to have faith in and love for the Living ECK Master and to accept him as teacher and guide. This carries them further and further along the path to God, the way to God-enlightenment. Only through the Living ECK Master can they be free of the physical universe, in which all events and things will swing from positive to negative and back again. These are the children who will be in control of themselves and events in the future. They will be prepared to be masters of their destinies and not the effect of people and situations.

With the younger minds and the youth today, very few of them have that struggle that an older person will have because they have been more flexible. They haven't been taught as stringently or as some of us who have had a very narrow upbringing.

I think of it in degrees. I wondered about that recently. I've always talked about my mother having a 10-degree viewpoint and my father, maybe a 190-degree, and it kept things pretty equal for me anyway. Maybe not the rest of the children in the family. But when we go through life and if we have been given the ability to choose ourself, within reason (under the guidance of your father and mother), do we want to eat this or eat that? Now, that's all that is prepared on the table, so sometimes if I didn't like that particular type of meat, I just ate bread and potatoes. I was happy with it. I had a choice. This is what I'm talking about. Without drumming in the fear of the negative factor "you should do this, you should do that"—this is what is being handed down through time. It is a guilt factor that has been impressed upon society throughout the world, not just one part of the world.

Those of you that are parents and have children taking some music lesson or some form of artistic work, sculpture, etc., and if their teacher says to do it this way but the youngster does it another, let them express themselves.

Sooner or later they will come out with something that might be of value, perhaps not to the parent, but to that individual later in life. Sometimes we can learn from others but if we force it, it can be dangerous to us. It wants to be free and easy. This substance that is known as Spirit (we call it ECK) if IT wants to go in another direction, and it is not the direction you wish to go in, let IT be. It isn't easy sometimes to let go and live life and let others be. Those that come to know the ECK know that they have a far greater love that is always with them.

In the little handbook Sri Paul Twitchell wrote for the ECK parent, *Your Children and the ECK Discourses,* one of the basic secrets that we can teach our children, I don't care what type of home they come from, is to teach them not to be for or against anything. But allow them to have their opinion. Listen to them. Even though they make a mistake, thank them. Thank them and they'll look at you and think:"What's the matter with mother or father?" And then you can show them very kindly, sometimes sternly, why the effects happened in the way they did, and they'll start to listen and trust you more openly.

Sing gentle songs to them. For children from

fifteen months on up to three (for the minds of the third and fourth year child are more developed and more receptive and open to ways of teaching them), we are forming their whole livelihood throughout life at this tender age. So love is one of the greater factors you can use. Getting down to the material things of life, see that their toys are colorful, that they have the opportunity to look at a lot of colored pictures, and listen to them when they find a picture that they like, that they express some interest in, but then go on to something else.

I know there are moments when a little child might do something wrong, when we reach for the brush right away, or give them our hand, then not meanfully but sometimes with love, and that's not necessarily wrong. But in the house where there are so many delicate things, they should be put out of reach. That child can learn later in life not to touch this or that. But at that young age, I'd say you would start to drive him into that clay shell and keep him there and imbed within that child that virtue of goodness and put them off-balance. They must be allowed to express themselves outwardly also.

If we can be as flexible as the children are; if we have a little blow-up with another person, okay, let it be. Don't hang on to it. Don't stay with that person's frustrations or that other person's situation. Then you can have and live that little happier life. If he's got himself into some web, that's his problem not yours.

If we can teach our children some music, as they're growing up at their mother's knee, and in our schools, not just an appreciation of it, but let the child choose whether to take up an instrument, or to sing, but the part that troubles me deeply is that in a good majority of our schools today, the children don't have the ability to pick up an instrument of their choice or some form of music because of the expense involved. It seems that the children that come from rich families are the fortunate ones. Many times they will be forced into it without their own individual choice. And one that has a deep desire to either become a composer or an artist in some form does not have the opportunity. And I know that in our school system there will be more help by those who are talented to work with the children. I know that in some schools that this has taken place. Some ECKists are going into the schools working with young children, high school, and even in the colleges, and giving of their time. While, as I've mentioned, some schools, where the music teachers and the chorus, are allowing the children to write and compose and produce their own works, it's fantastic. As a rule it's very enjoyable. Because the children of today, and those who are writing the music, are the ones that are really responsible for the music of tomorrow. Yet, it can be enjoyed today, in the here and now.

I don't think my father read a note; and it's been twenty years since I have. But he had in our house a half dozen instruments, or more. And all my mother could do is whistle and play the harmonica a little bit. But there was always some music, and of course, the blues as well.

I have a brief note that I'd like to share with you. A young lady was asking for help, and it shows you how man, through his educational processes, gets wrapped up in the world consciousness, brings about strife and inner turmoil for us individually, sometimes whether we are in school or at work, could be even at play.

This young lady was stressed quite terribly by her children being forced, or told they were going to get a poor grade at school if they don't go out here and (what some people say today) "hawk" a squirrel; that means kill a squirrel, or collect 60 bugs for their class.

The note says: "Can you help me with a subject that has been disturbing my children and myself? In high school they are studying earth sciences and have been told that in order to pass they have to either get a bug collection of at least 60 to mount or kill and mount a squirrel. It seems to me that there must be another method of observing nature and wildlife than to go out and kill and step into the balance of God's nature. There must be another method of teaching than to have to kill. My children don't understand this method and don't want to do it, and will probably fail this required course because the killing part of it is 70% of the grade."

Now I'm not saying it's right or wrong, but what are we teaching our children in school? There was a time in this country when it was necessary to go out and hunt and get some food to feed the family, whether it was turkey, deer, various other animals. That's a different sort of circumstances and situation. When it's not necessary, the law of nature takes care of itself which is wrapped up in the world consciousness.

Those of us who are human beings must go beyond that into the God-conscious plane, the pure positive God Worlds. It's not easy. In this world consciousness, some of us as human beings tend to put the animals into the God-planes of existence and it isn't up to us as individuals to determine that. That's up to the Lords of Karma. There's an ECK Master that's associated with that kingdom. Even though an animal will have a Soul, it's possible, (I'm not saying it's true for all) but it's possible that if an animal is run over accidentally by an automobile or some other means, that part of that bird or animal might be taken beyond the lower worlds into the higher realms.

Chapter 8

THE KEY TO SELF-SURRENDER

I wish to take up a very controversial subject, one called self-surrender. A very few people know what this phrase means. Generally, the attitude toward self-surrender can be divided into three parts: those who have a blurred idea of it, those who have a mental concept of it, those who have a feeling of it. But none of these are actually self-surrender.

Self-surrender is the real key to spiritual success in the heavenly worlds. If one is looking for success on any plane in the invisible world, this is the way, for only by self-surrender do we gain illumination and knowledge of true spirituality. And, of course, entrance into the Kingdom of God.

The question that arises in the mind—to whom does one surrender? The surrender is to the Inner Master, of course, not to the physical form that is seen with the outer eyes but to the Living ECK Master who comes to you in the radiant form.

Surrender to the Inner Master is one of the most paradoxical principles which faces everyone who is trying to enter the higher realms of the deity. Almost every true devotee of God becomes frantic and desperately strives to reach the ultimate goal, or receive some light on his problem, without surrendering. This serves only to increase his frustration. There is only one way that is practiced universally among the mystics and God-intoxicated. This way is simple, but so much of a primary source that we are apt to overlook it. It is the way of the daring, the patient and enterprising and ambitious.

The Inner Master can be found by sitting in

silence while one is doing the spiritual contemplative exercise and gazing into the spiritual eye, not striving, not pushing, but by gentle patience. Eventually, the light will come like a curtain around the watcher and the inner ear opens for the sound. Often, there is a slow rocking of the body as if it were in a rocking chair. After this, the Inner Master, or what we know as the Spiritual Traveler, steps into the area of the spiritual eye and takes the watcher out of the physical consciousness into the invisible planes.

This is simple so far, but it is not self-surrender to the radiant form of the Spiritual Traveler, the Inner Master. One can have the Spiritual Traveler in his life but not surrender to him. This is the paradoxical nature of God and it runs through our lives like a thread from the physical situation to the higher experiences. One may have God in his life, but not have him. One may have the Inner Master, or the Spiritual Traveler, in his life, but again perhaps the Inner Master may not have you. If we study this paradox, it will easily resolve itself. It is basically placing the attention on the Inner Self, for this Inner Master is actually Spirit, known as ECK. And the form is that whom we know in the Outer, teaching us the path to the Far Country.

The release of all tensions and conflicts is the first step to self-surrender, turning all difficulties and problems over to this Inner Master and, of course, turning your inner life over to him also. It is when anyone can come to this stage that we know Spirit (Inner Master) has taken over and controls and guides him in the path to the SUGMAD. It takes care of all problems with his material world and takes care of any possible situation which might arise on the inner planes. This is a knowing beyond the ken of the senses, a conception beyond the sense

48

world. One can never explain or tell what it is, but must lean upon the intuitive knowledge that I am Spirit and Spirit is me. It is actually this simple, and by becoming the instrument through which Spirit flows so rapidly, one is able to accomplish deeds beyond his expectations, find self-healing, and the ability to help others in all fields. He will find himself able to ride the spiritual currents and cross to heaven to the very realm of dying, and return to the physical form that is left below on the lower material plane.

Giving up to the Inner Master, the Spiritual Traveler of ECK, whichever you wish to call it, is not letting go of free will but making use of it for the Divine Cause. The attention is put upon the inner form of the teacher and therefore one plans according to the instruction and wisdom received from the inner planes. This is where the creative faculty and free will are put to use, like all other faculties of man. These have comparable faculties on the inner planes and the power flows through these to the objective faculty, the physical mind.

If one sits in silence, waiting for the Spiritual Traveler to come and take him into the cosmic world, he will likely meet with disappointment. Therefore, he must put his free will to use in determining where he would like to go under the gentle guidance of the Spiritual Traveler and what might be expected. If it is right for you to take the journey to the plane of your desire, your will can be fulfilled. But it takes the use of creative faculty of Spirit to plan and measure out what might be before you in the cosmic world. The law is that everything is in accordance to your experience and your belief in the higher world.

Those that have problems or can come to that place on the path and step to the side should understand Self-Surrender, for any difficulties one has are always created by his own thoughts as well as actions.

Chapter 9

ECK AND THE OCCULT

The occult is practiced by literally millions who are not aware they're interfering with another person's state of consciousness, but there is no occult practice that can affect those in ECK.

There is so much that comes to me in letters from people who get into an area of depression or they're headed down in spirits and they don't recall or remember how they can lift themselves out of this into that state of Spirit. They don't remember how to once again have that freedom not only of choice, but an inner freedom emotionally. It's a stability.

A lot of this not only comes from our own thoughts but is impressed upon us from those around us. It's practiced by literally millions throughout the world who are not aware they're interfering with another person's state of consciousness.

The practice of the occult, whether it be by an individual or a group, is what we want to talk about; because individuals must have some sort of shield or protection in order to ward it off and be able to handle any psychic attack, whether it be subtle or open.

Now the ECKist has this shield whether he realizes it or not, regardless of who he is or where he is at on the path, or what level of spiritual unfoldment he has reached. This protection is in the form of a globe of light, and if you use it, another person's thought cannot affect you or sway you. We as individuals must make up our own minds and within ourselves make the decisions pertaining to our outer life and how we live it.

There are a number of different ways in which man uses the occult not only to sway others but the masses in general — and it filters down to each individual whether it's through the medium of radio or television or in the form of music. If it is used rightly for the good of all, there seems to be no problem. But when it is not used rightly for the good of all or the good of the whole, then there are always difficulties and problems.

The practice of the occult is very often subtle. It's not just as in voodoo, building a little doll and sticking a pin in it. It can be done mentally. An individual can, through mind control, attempt to control others. We know this. This is nothing new. But there are those who aren't affected by it.

When another individual might pray for you or think or feel that something is good for you, whether it be an occupation or a piece of clothing, or food, you can reject it if you feel to, whether it's spoken verbally or silently. If you aren't at that point of spiritual unfoldment to know this is happening or this has happened, but you suspect it, don't jump to conclusions, ask for that guidance.

The function of the spiritual guide for those in ECKANKAR is that no individual needs to be lonely who is on this path. And if one realizes what he's got going for himself, there is no occult practice in this world, or any other world, that can affect him as an individual here in this physical plane. And those individuals who can move Spirit through prayer or meditation, they cannot touch you.

The many occult practices that are in this world are carryovers from the old country, from the East and from man's early form of survival. He had a family, a good piece of country or land, whether it was for tilling, or had an abundance of animals, and he had to protect it in some way. Stones and spears were limited and he learned that by certain forms of thought he could protect not only his family, but his whole property. In a sense this is a form of the occult, an occult practice, and it is used quite extensively today.

There is real danger for those who take up the study of the occult without a competent spiritual master. ESP, clairvoyance, witchcraft, hypnotism, demonology or contacting the spirits of the deceased can certainly lead to a breakdown or degradation of those who participate, homicides and mental cases.

Man in his ego always believes that he can outwit or manipulate the negative forces. It always appears this way because the negative wants to establish the illusion that man is the greatest of all in this world. But in the end, man usually finds himself in a mental institution or in other disastrous situations.

Chapter 10

MUSIC, THE FUEL FOR SOUL

Music is fuel for Soul, like the old saying, "Music is the meat of Soul" but it is fuel for Soul. I enjoy all types of music and there is good and bad in everything, including music.

It is possible to impose on someone's psychic space without them even knowing it; however, most people that have any degree of awareness will be aware of it and will do something about it. Yet as a whole, it can happen without that person knowing about it. An excellent example is the outbreaks in France. On weekends they have had dances with rock music and this is usually attended by a lot of young people. There have been a lot of murders and various sorts of accidents associated with it, and it seems at some point of the evening, some person is triggered by the music who goes berserk because he has had too much to drink or has taken some drug.

I have seen that happen in this country and in other parts of the world as well. This can also be accomplished with certain types of symphonic music, not just rock, certain types of jazz, called discordant music.

Certain types of music, in time, can change these patterns and it can be most alarming to the consciousness. Many times this subtlety takes place moments, days, or years later, patterns that are built up. Each of us carry this magnetic field about us and within that structure certain patterns are formed.

The first thing that strikes a newcomer to jazz is he looks at the history and the people that have made up the jazz world, in a sense its mythology. It is so involved with self-destruction. Jazz history is extraordinary, dramatic, and it started deep in the South and has grown to what it is today. Yet man tends to forget the early instruments, the sounds that he can produce to aid himself for healing, not only uplifting the spirit. It is true, music is the meat of Soul.

Music is very powerful, a very powerful force in the world. People do not realize it but music can influence a person to do good or evil things. That is why every note I play, sing, write or chord structure, I try to make it a note of love, to counterbalance the various evil forces in this world, not just emanating from music but there are many avenues through which the Kal (negative force) works.

Rock music is getting very angry, destructive, and evil. It is almost a devil worship for the youth. It becomes very angry and destructive to society as a whole. The ECK music is the only sane music in man's society.

Tibetan music is very discordant. It doesn't fit the western world, yet some of the music lovers enjoy it. Blues have always been a part of music. I have mentioned at a seminar about my experience with a single noted flute off the Soul plane. It was very beautiful, haunting, melodious, uplifting, yet it is a blues sound.

There are differences of opinion about instruments and its arrangement and its use. A guitar that is amplified is not really considered electronic, for the voice is amplified just as a guitar is, or an accordion, a harp, a vibra-harp, a violin. I prefer to hear the better sounds — the strings, the woodwinds, the flutes. Those instruments that can harmonize and bring forth a power of positive feeling, music that will be uplifting and assuring to

Soul, that will reach Soul.

The influence of music is more powerful and continuous than that of other arts because of the factor of repetition. One may attend a play once or twice in a legitimate theater and then have the feeling he has exhausted its meaning. The same is true for a good book, other than the books on ECKANKAR and its teachings, for one can read *The Shariyat-Ki-Sugmad, The Spiritual Notebook, The Flute of God,* or *Stranger by the River* many times and each time will get something new from it.

To return daily to contemplate a certain painting in a gallery, or a piece of sculpture, it wouldn't last. We would tire of it. Once the symbolism of that has been impressed upon the mind, we are satisfied and seek elsewhere for further stimulation of the senses. In the case of music, however, the reaction is entirely different. One can hear the same piece repeatedly and seldom tire of it. One can attend concert after concert and each time you can feel an enlargement of understanding and the original pleasure is renewed and intensified. Music lovers the world over have heard selections of Beethoven and Bach hundreds of times without tiring of the harmonies and the melodies.

It seems like the secret of ECK lies in the fact that music is invisible and therefore does not immediately reveal its full significance. We weary of forms more frequently because they impose upon us the full pictures of themselves. They invite acceptance on a level of preachment or teachment. They tell us what they mean. Whereas music draws persuasively upon our own understanding. We must give of ourselves to music if we are to share in its meaning. This is not understood by all, including ECKists. Yet ECKists really are closer to this than most people. In fact, the ECKist is often inspired to create and bestow meaning from within oneself, although we hear the same selections at some of the seminars and on various occasions, there is always a difference. Because in the passing of time and the various ways of living, each of us become different in our thought and understanding. The countless changes in our old psychic life causes old music to seem new sometimes. But that which is created by the ECKist and by the new writers of the day will seem to adjust themselves to our immediate requirements. Thus, understand that music is friendly, lovable and intimate. I'm speaking of the music that is sweet, that is harmonious and uplifting, that is not harsh and hard. We can turn to it both in joy and sorrow and find it forever gracious.

The ECK and Its religion of the individual self is not long-faced nor gloomy. It is the greatest source of true happiness. It is the only music. The ECKist should take upon himself the task of developing a capacity for happiness. We should not be like a woman who lived next door to my folks' house. She wore a sun bonnet that extended some inches beyond her face and when asked one day by my mother why she wore it, it was lest she should see something to make her laugh. A part of her idea of being a Christian was refraining from laughter.

Now others while not so extreme, think it is a mark of spirituality to be grave, dignified, and shut out of life whatever would make it bright, cheerful and happy. Now remember, the survival factors in these lower worlds of duality are a bright attitude, a cheerful surrounding, honest laughter and happiness.

Not too long ago when I was a little boy I was determined to be happy. I had seen unhappiness as a child in different walks of life, not only in my family and loved ones, but outside of the family circle and in life. I was fortunate to have the ability to travel and see different parts of the world and the unhappiness, the long faces that exist.

I am happy every day! I will not be any other way! I have had my troubles, as many of them as most of you had. I have learned that troubles do not make unhappiness; it is only the wrong attitude toward a situation or difficulty. Any trouble we are faced with is caused from ourselves unless it is impressed upon us by others.

If you are busy being glad
    and trying to cheer others who are sad
Although your heart may ache
    you will soon forget to notice it
    and you will be glad.

Today singers and other entertainers use the words *soul music, soul food,* and other things which are only for the emotional and physical senses. What is usually being said is that "feeling" is "soul." This is hardly anything more than the psychic element of life or what we know as emotion, generated from the second plane of life, known in the esoteric language as the astral world. It is of little spiritual value and generally misleads those who are exposed to its influences through music, dialogue and physical encounter. This has nothing to do with the actual spiritual nature of man, for this sort of person is not aware of the meaning of Soul.

A good example is what has happened to those in the world of entertainment and the movie industry who believed they could flaunt the laws of the psychic worlds. Many well-known figures have become drug addicts, neurotics, paranoids, and even suicides. Such people can influence those who are looking for an idol to worship, usually in any mass society. The hero is taken from any element of life regardless of whether he is a warrior, musician or film producer.

Soul means *spiritual awareness,* developing the perception of knowing and seeing or spiritual unfoldment, the attainment of the true spiritual insight. One sees and knows through the divine senses within. It is hypocritical and without foundation for true devotion to label anything commercial with such sacred words as *Soul* which we have traditionally used for the uplifting of the individual to higher worship and thinking.

In America and other countries of the world, people believe that Blues came from the colored people. This is not right. It comes from the Soul plane, from the heavenly worlds.

We have the happy, cheerful Blues that are uplifting and we have the melancholy Blues originating out of the hard work that one has to do or the problems and troubles of our lives.

Rock and roll is the expression of the lower power. I used to play good jazz vibes, but I've changed, not so much the structure, for some aspects of jazz are very creative. It's as creative as symphonic music if it's done tastefully. Take the Modern Jazz Quartet. They do some beautiful things. But that which has a hard jungle beat is from the jungle, in a sense. It pokes holes in individuals' auras just as certain negative aspects with drugs do.

The musicians on the planet Venus think that their music is greater than ours, that is, if you can see them with your physical eyes. But in the same respect the music out of the mental worlds, once it's heard, you won't want to listen to the Earth music or to the music of Venus. Once you hear the five melodies of ECK or the music off the Soul plane or the haunting flute off the Soul plane, the single noted flute, you don't want to hear any other music than that which derives from the pure positive God Worlds.

You lose all your taste for music and yet when you're living here you must live amongst other people. I enjoy the symphonic music and a good jazz group that doesn't have a hard beat to it but that plays and sounds more softly. I love music because music is that of sound, a light in itself that we know as Light and Sound. All things are manifested by them.

Coming back one morning into the physical realm out of nowhere, the ECK presented a choir of voices, both male and female, a choir which I have never heard. I thought it to be the physical, but it was very subtle; you might call it celestial sounds without a rhythm, without a beat.

Electronic music is as bad as the drums. It's manufactured. The human being can become a vehicle for Spirit and if you're expressing yourself artistically or with words or with music, machines cannot do that. It can only do that which it has been programmed to do.

Spirit transmits through your fingers and you get down to the low notes of the piano, for instance, or the spectrum of the scale and it sets up a psychological feeling within the human body. You can disturb the physiological aspect of man through sound. But if you go beyond that which cannot be made mechanically, Spirit takes over and it can still be felt. The same thing is true at the high end of the spectrum. They are still sounds that I can hear or a person can hear that becomes attuned to it or you can feel it with the inner ear.

Music goes beyond words. It speaks straight to our heart and reaches the very core and root of Soul. Music soothes us, stirs us up. It puts noble feelings in us. It melts us to tears at times. Yet we know not how it works. It is the language that, by itself, is divine.

Chapter 11

AWAKENING OF THE CONSCIOUSNESS

Most of the young folks out there in the world
that have any yearning for spiritual development
may go to church. The ECKists sometimes get up
before going to work and go to a far greater temple.
It is very interesting that so few understood in the
time of Jesus. They didn't truly understand the
temple he was talking about. He was very clear in
his words about the temple of stone that he tried to
have the people not remove, but to develop their
awareness about the outer temple that they were
going to and tie this directly to the inner temple.

It is from there and only there that one can
expand his consciousness, which is essential. In
doing this, it is around the heart area. It can be very
small or as big as your room, but it doesn't matter.
The thing that is important is the individual having
this experience, this awakening of the consciousness. The shifting of the consciousness is very easy
and it is automatic once you learn how to do it.

We go around seeking the spiritual food in the
physical and until we find it we are always looking.
I am not saying that when you step on this path of
ECK that it is going to end immediately for you.
Those who have doubts, relax, and don't let anyone
pull the wool over your eyes, because the doubts are
healthy. I don't think that there was a greater
doubter than myself. The older Initiates or individuals in ECK know that Sri Paul Twitchell himself said that he too was a doubter. This is construc-
tive, to be shown in some manner, whether it is in
the form of light on the inner plane or objectively to

61

have that experience through a vision.

Many of our present religions have been built on a vision. They do not understand that this is within the lower worlds only. Whether it is off the astral or the mental world, let them worship if they choose to. Whether it is through meditation, prayer or even if it is a leaf or a rock. This worshipping is not to be taken lightly; it's personal. It is something that you don't demonstrate to others nor to the loved ones because they won't understand you. If you are not being understood, then friction arises. This friction is caused from the lack of understanding of those around you, sometimes within yourself as a human being. It happens to me occasionally; I forgot to get out of the human state of consciousness into the God-consciousness state.

The ECK of Itself chooses us as individuals whether it is to read a book or to step on the path of ECK with the knowledge that is gained for that individual who chooses to be a vehicle for the SUGMAD, there are many trials and tribulations to go through or tests as they are known. I do not test you in the physical or on the other side unless I am directed to. Then usually it is the ECK or Lords of Karma.

This outer life in the clay shell is for you to take care of. You are given the guidance help and spiritual protection. But the direction, whether it is in the dream state or spiritual contemplative exercises, is for your development in the Soul body in working your way through the physical, astral, causal, mental worlds and then into the Soul plane. If you follow your intuitiveness and develop that to a greater degree, then your perceptiveness or perception on the inner planes, as well as out here, becomes far greater.

This is being able to see things with your physical

eyes or with your spiritual eye, not to analyze, but know what you have seen taking place, to have that understanding. The understanding that one gets and gains, whether it is about himself, his loved one, or this world, or the Far Country, can lead to greater spiritual heights. It is experienced in the Soul body and it filters through to the physical sometimes. And sometimes the trouble that one gets into on the astral plane or mental worlds filter through to the physical body.

The individual that takes on the responsibility of mastership for himself, goes through all sorts of trials and it is to see whether or not you can handle the responsibility. It takes indifference to certain situations, detachment from other things, humility and love. To be humble takes a lot of discipline of one's self, but it also takes some experience, experience with the Light and Sound, and complete understanding. In the physical body and mind, you cannot have complete and total understanding of the pure positive God Worlds. A great deal of individuals throughout the world do not bring back to the human state of consciousness everything that they would like to. Some forget that of every action and through every experience, as well as the teachings in the Wisdom Temples that are taught to the ECKists, they have a complete record.

For the majority of us, many times, we are not shown or are aware of these classes, but during the day or in the dream state after a class, this flood of knowledge and information pours in. It is at that time that the cup is turned up and you can hold it.

In any occupation it takes a certain amount of imagination and a certain amount of initiative to become greater. I believe Rebazar Tarzs told Sri Paul Twitchell in *The Key to ECKANKAR* to "become lost in what you are doing at any moment of time." This is what happens to a musician or an artist; they forget. They shut off the world and get lost for those moments that they are putting a picture on the canvas or a piece of music down. Otherwise, there are too many things pulling at you and you are unable to do the work with feeling which is required.

This can be designing a dress or an electronic device or doing something creative on the farm. This is getting lost in yourself and what you are doing in that moment of time. And if you bring up things from yesterday or what somebody said two months ago or what happened, you are distracting that action that you are trying to have take place or that thought in that creative moment. Even if it is adding up some figures, to get it right every time, you have to have your attention on what you are doing.

It takes a little bit of constantness and has nothing to do with concentration. It is applying only the thought of what you are doing at the moment without letting other things distract you mentally. Now this takes some time to do. It is very necessary, first on the outer, to have a little experience of getting lost with yourself in that moment of time in what you are doing and getting wrapped up in it without letting other things bug you, or other people, whether it is their actions or their thoughts. We find that in the world today we can walk down the street and other individuals' thoughts are impressed upon us if we let them and they sway us many times into their way of thinking. You have got to be an individual and think for yourself without letting others do it for you.

When you have that feeling of "well, I should do this or that," and you don't know, take advantage and do what you think is right for yourself at that moment. Too many hesitate. That old saying is "he who hesitates is lost," but it takes some common sense not to go off too far on a tangent. If a person is able to get lost in the moment of time in what he is doing whether he is at work or at play, then he can start to have some greater control, of what is happening within himself.

Many forget about the ethics involved in life. Whether it is to yourself, your loved ones or those that you deal with in the outer world, living the life of ECK we are supposed to have the highest code of ethics. If you don't, I guess it is all right too. Because it is a responsibility that the individual must take upon himself, and if you see somebody with very loose morals or other forms that society thinks are unethical, don't judge him. Let him stumble over his own blocks—he will. Because you or I or anyone else cannot judge another person. We leave that to the nine Silent Ones or the SUGMAD ITSELF, the ECK. The ECK knows what is best for us and what we need at the moment.

You can lift up those around you without interfering with their state of consciousness, by letting the ECK, the Living ECK Master, assist you whether at work or at play or just day-dreaming. And those day-dreams are very necessary.

If we make a game out of getting out of the lower worlds, you will find that you have a little more happiness occasionally. It is a very serious step to take when you step onto this Path of ECKANKAR. It is the greatest one you can take in this lifetime. And if you only get the second initiation, fine. We are going to have some that will get their twelfth too.

The ECK is going to reach those who are ready for it, those who have the ears to hear. Those who are seeking, but haven't the eyes to see, will see through many of you that are here now.

Sri Paul Twitchell referred to an excellent spiritual exercise called "The Easy Way" which appears on page 90 of *In My Soul I Am Free,* Brad Steiger's book about Paul. Paul states: "One of the simple techniques which I have developed over the years is one I call 'The Easy Way.' Just before going to bed at night, sit in an easy chair or on the floor, back erect, and concentrate the attention on the spiritual eye, that place between the eyebrows, while chanting the AUM, or God, inwardly and silently. Hold the attention on a black screen in the inner vision, and keep it free from any pictures if at all possible. If you need a substitute for any mental pictures flashing up unwantedly, place the image of Christ, or some saint, or a holy man that you know, in place of them.

"After a few minutes of this, suddenly there will come a faint clicking sound in one ear, or the sound of a cork popping, and you will find yourself outside the body looking back at the physical one in the room and ready for a short journey in the other worlds.

"There is nothing to fear, for no harm can come to you while outside the body, nor to it when left behind. A teacher or guru will be standing by, although you may not know it, to keep watch over your progress. After awhile the spirit body will return and slide gently into the body with hardly more than a very light jolt. If not successful the first time, try it again, for the technique works. It has worked for others."

By regular daily use of this spiritual exercise, one can establish the inner relationship with Spirit essential to becoming a vehicle for Spirit to use. By learning to place attention upon the inner self, Soul, one's true reality is fine-tuned, awakened and sharpened to the realization of Its purpose for being. The necessity of these spiritual exercises, those inward travels with the Inner Master, cannot be stressed strongly enough. They should be continued through the higher initiations in ECKANKAR to maintain a healthy inflow and outflow of Spirit within the ECKist. If this flow is allowed to stagnate from unuse, the individual will experience difficulties he cannot explain or relate to. Like a dam, built to hold quantities of water, an outflow or overflow outlet must be provided to channel out what comes in or the dam may burst, unable to handle what it has received.

Chapter 12

A NEW LOOK AT THE SUN

The earth is encircled by different sheaths, let's say, which serve different functions. Outermost are gamma rays in a wave frequency, interlocking with the magnetic lines of flux, which are another wave frequency running perpendicular to the other. This magnetic line is the voltage, in a sense, in this energy loop.

The dark sun spots are the areas of the sun from which most of the energy is emitted to this planet and the rest of the solar system. Every eleven years there is a change in the sun spot cycle and they become more powerful. The "donut" that surrounds the earth, known as the Van Allen radiation belt, absorbs and stores the energy and in turn supports the earth and sustains it magnetically.

Now getting into the core of the earth, there are two levels usually spoken of. Science thinks of the outer core as molten, probably of a nickel-iron substance, and the inner core as solid. The inner core, however, is also molten. So now the question is, what makes the warmth on the surface of the earth?

Well, it is not from the rays of the sun. Instead it is a magnetic function set up between the factors we have been talking about. In summer, the sun is actually *further* away from the hemisphere, that is, in that season, and the effect is like stretching tension on a rubber band. The energy lines joining the sun and the earth's current sheaths set up a magnetic function on the core of the earth which draws the molten core into action to that side of the earth. The reason it is warmer in summer is because of the increased work of the energy taking place inside the earth and towards the crust of the earth. It's a magnetic function. In the winter it is the complete opposite. There's less work force or energy that's taking place near the crust. So it is the position of the planet in relation to the magnetic field that creates the seasons, and the temperature change from night to day. The equator is always warm because it isn't affected by the tilt of the earth's axis and always maintains the same position in relation to the magnetic field.

The sun is quite a source of energy that man has at his disposal that he is not using yet; he's going about it in the wrong way. There is a great misunderstanding that the sun itself is hot, but it isn't true. If you take a prism or a defraction grating, and look into the sun, the break-up of the light into different colors, what you are seeing is always in existence throughout the universes. What you are seeing as colors are unmanifested Souls (which science speaks of as atoms) in different rates of frequency, or, you might say, states of consciousness. This relates to the colors seen in an individual's aura and also the colors found in the spiritual universes. You're viewing a small part of the Audible Life Stream, the ECK, made up of the same atoms we inhale and that give life. It's called the Ocean of Love and Mercy.

Now the sun receives its energy from the same source that supports and sustains all life, known as ECK, and the attraction of living things to the sun is the same as Soul being drawn to the spiritual light found on the inner planes. They are made of the same substance, though at a different rate of frequency. It is the ECK only. These atoms, unmanifested Souls, can be ignited at any moment of time, anywhere, in any galaxy, universe or part of heaven.

This is a source of energy, in a sense, which we can draw upon and use. On Venus they use the magnetic lines of flux to motivate their vehicles through space, and this is not misusing Spirit. Rather man is misusing it with the varieties of internal combustion engines, which waste fuel and harm the environment. He hasn't yet found the key to unlocking the energy readily at his disposal.

It's interesting, though man's science would not agree, but beyond the outer cover, the outer sheath, on the main body of the sun, there is life there too.

When man sends a vehicle into outer space many times the aura that covers the planet is punctured. Those who are aware observe that every time a space mission takes place there is something happening on this planet of a negative nature. It lets more negative current flow through that aura.

The same thing happens with us as individuals by letting negative thoughts go out from us. It will puncture the outermost sheath. Certain words or thoughts are more detrimental to this effect of puncturing the astral body because it must go from the mental on through the outer sheaths which are basically electromagnetic in structure, the atom structure, each at a different rate of vibration. You as an individual can close these gaps or holes through the spiritual exercises.

We find that those having a better health seem to be greater in traveling the path of ECKANKAR. If you haven't got good health, it's very difficult. Yet, that doesn't mean that you are going to be held back in growing spiritually. There is a great misunderstanding there.

The health factor goes along with thoughts of joy and your attitude of non-resistance to whatever happens, keeping that happy attitude within yourself, and that cheerfulness. These are factors of survival in the Far Country.

The mind wants to get us into various corners, wants to chew on certain things, and we have a hold of something like a crab and won't let go. We have to take our attention off that which we want. The person has to let the stream of thought run through the mind as a river. And in doing so we must not catch the fish in their rivers. Be very observant by not being a bystander, but being active and part of that. Because life must be lived in the physical body here on this plane of existence.

If one realizes that self-surrender is giving up the little things about others or about yourself, the back-biting or chewing over things, he will find that knowledge and that wisdom about the Far Country.

A polarization of the atoms takes place when the sun is out, and it produces warmth. The same thing is true when the Living ECK Master of the time is amongst chelas, whether in the physical or radiant body, there is polarization of the atom structure and they feel that warmth and love. In the shade the unmanifested atoms are not polarized, but when the sun is present in view they are. There is a particular energy, work force, that takes place. The light photon and the properties of the light are actually what activates the polarization.

If the ECKist recognizes this, and places his attention on the Living ECK Master at the time of need or stress or anytime, that polarization will take place. Then he could be in a dark spot and be warm, or in trouble and know that he is being guided through it, or going through a rough area whether it is physical or spiritual.

71

Chapter 13

SCIENCE AND ECKANKAR

This planet is basically the ashcan of the universe. It is a training ground as are any of the other planets that sustain life. Yet the evolution of the individuals on these other planets or galaxies are a little further advanced than Man on this planet. There is a doctor down at Salk Institute in the San Diego area who believes that man was planted on this planet Earth from other worlds or other planets and to some degree he's correct. Yet there's a good number of people that are living here today that have been on this planet for more lifetimes than I'd even want to say.

There is a great deal of interest in this area today because Man's scriptures speak of beings coming from out of the sky or from out of machines or vehicles that were foreign to them in that period of time, then returned to the sky.

Essentially my role as the Living ECK Master is the same regardless of what planet or plane of existence, whether it is a planet in the physical universe such as Venus, or the astral, causal or mental planes. For the individuals that reside there, whether it's on Earth or another planet, or a dimension within time and space such as the astral or mental worlds, my only concern is that that person who is ready or desires during this lifetime, who wants to experience, wants to get back to the God-state, has that opportunity.

There is a statue in Japan that looks almost like a Buddha, that supposedly was brought to this planet from Venus about 6,000 years ago. Although the teachings of ECKANKAR were handed down from Venus to Earth, the teachings of ECK and ITS origin initiated from the Soul plane. There is a Golden Wisdom Temple on each of the planes from the Soul plane down through the mental world, the causal, astral and finally down to the physical plane of existence. One of these Wisdom Temples is on the planet Venus and there are two others in the physical world.

As the lower worlds were constructed, a Wisdom Temple also was constructed and ultimately filtered through the physical world as Soul was sent to the various levels of existence for development or spiritual experience. That is all we are here for.

There are a number of people that were responsible for "seeding" the Earth. During the time of Atlantis, they had machines that could do interplanetary travel and this is nothing new for those minds that are open, those individuals who say, "Well, I'm neither for nor against it, but the possibility exists."

The spiritual travelers on the Path of ECKANKAR are able to manifest themselves in any world, anywhere on this planet and in any one of the planes of existence. We have a number of ECKists today that are also reaching that point, and we have some Fifth Initiates and Higher who are in the physical body, who take care of their daily responsibilities, hold a Satsang Class or Discussion Group, and are also teaching on the astral, causal and mental planes. As they develop and become adept in what is known as Soul Travel, they will reach one day the point where they, at their own volition, are able to be in several places at the same time.

Many wouldn't believe the length of time that the spiritual travelers have been on this planet and in this universe and the thousands of years they have existed. In the great breakthroughs in science, normally the credit can be given to these spiritual travelers, while we in the physical are inclined to give the credit to the individual who may have uncovered it.

Some of the music I have written wasn't really my music. I just rearranged the notes that already exist yet I was the vehicle for that which is known as ECK to work through, to express.

That individual who is scientifically oriented becomes a vehicle also. But one can even gain out there greater awareness of himself and of the things in this world and expand his consciousness to reach into, whether it be the Museum of Science on the astral plane where all of man's inventions, past, present and future exist, or if he wants to go beyond that to uncovering this information for an individual.

Giving an example of my own experience: I came across this Museum not in astral projection but in evolving myself spiritually through Soul Travel and its techniques using Soul as a vehicle. I found that I could stay there half an hour (where through astral projection it's momentary), and to witness, to see what is going to be coming out from Man in the way of things that he'll use for himself and to make life easier on this Earth plane. It's fantastic!

After visiting the Museum of Science on the Astral plane, I came back with some new information and a new gadget that was what we call an electronic device and it wasn't supposed to function according to the law of physics. I took it to this patent attorney and he called his physicist in and he looked at it and shook his head. He couldn't understand it. The more I talked, the more confused he became because he did not understand its principle, yet he saw it work and marvelled at it. I was pestered not only by automobile companies and oil companies but by governments as well; it was too revolutionary, I wound up destroying the item.

If you come across something you can use it for your own ends, but how are you going to use it? If you can go to this place where all of Man's inventions are derived and you can come out with something new, you can make a bundle of money, retire and live a good life. But with that attitude, a person is very unlikely to be shown or be taken to the Museum of Science. But if the individual has his project in mind to aid mankind, to assist and is not greedy, is not doing it either for the money or the benefits he will reap out of it as an individual, then you can bring things through of a scientific nature.

Time exists within the lower worlds, the worlds from the etheric plane down to the physical world. There you can measure time, measure distances, you have a yardstick to go by that the physical mind can grasp and can relate to very easily. From the Soul plane on up into the pure positive God Worlds there is no time as we know time. Man knows nothing about these worlds of existence, but the teachings of ECKANKAR try to get the individual out of these lower worlds as swiftly as possible and into the worlds of pure positiveness where there is no time and space as we know it. The reason for this is that, that individual can then be able to have at his disposal a joy or be able to reach that bliss state that most people are seeking and are unable to. They are able to rise above time, space and matter in this manner, whether they are at work, at play or out on the street. When something takes place they are not affected by cause.

Everything in this physical world and within the succeeding worlds up to the etheric plane, including the planes beyond, vibrate at a specific rate or frequency. In medical science today Man is learning that he can use ultrasonics for correcting certain situations within the physical body, say a torn limb or a muscle; if the right ultrasonic frequency is directed at this area within the physical body, the cells are readjusted and the pain and discomfort is eliminated. The tissue and the muscles are corrected.

Now the healing that takes place via Soul Travel which one can learn to do himself, or if the request is made of myself and I appear to the individual, this is all I'm doing, adjusting the vibratory rate in that particular area of discomfort.

The Soul body vibrates, the highest rate of vibration that exists. Man does not really know it, it is not measurable. When one is able to move within the Soul body, then Soul is not moving, in essence, but the individual from his point of view is able to KNOW what is happening, whether he might be able to move from here to San Francisco or New York and see what is happening there. When one starts to gain some experience via Soul Travel in the Soul body, one doesn't move in the Soul body, one KNOWS. It's a vast difference.

Within the pure positive God Worlds is the area where creation, a greater creativity, exists than here or in any of the lower worlds. It is stressed in the ECK teachings that all creation is finished for the physical, astral, causal and mental planes of existence. The individual is able to either look into the future or the past at his own volition and know for himself what to do at the next moment of time or where he is going and what he is going to do and have confidence in what he is doing.

It has been known for a good number of years that Man has an aura and this is a sheath, an electromagnetic field basically, and within the aura are specific colors. If a person is angry he will show certain colors or change from one color to another and if he is continually using certain drugs or alcohol, it will show another color within that electromagnetic spectrum or aura. Understanding this is a start for many people to what is called self-realization.

One reaches the point on the spiritual ladder of life when he must give up everything on the inner within himself as well as on the outer, and this does not mean that you give up your home, your automobile or that sort of thing but being attached, and this attachment must be given up.

When a young man or woman is growing up, parents do not wish to turn loose of them. They hang on to them and try to live their lives for them, in the sense that they tell them what to wear, what they should eat, what kind of friends they should have. These inner attachments to things and people must be given up and to situations as well. ECKANKAR teaches that we don't have to practice austerities; you can have your things in the world and use the technology that man has to help himself.

The use of the term "science" occurred in Gopal Das' time in Egypt and prior to that in the early period of this planet as well as on other planets. Through investigation one takes upon himself, if he wants to know about some certain physical object, its foundation or why it happens in a certain way, you have to take it in steps, break it down. If it's an electromechanical device, it takes electrical energy to make it move, but making it move electrically there's a mechanical function that happens.

This is basic physics, but there is the scientific part of it. If you are investigating something that goes against the laws of mathematics that are set by Man and established by Man, we call it scientific.

The unknown, investigating the unknown, is an aspect of the science. One finds that ECKANKAR is a very exacting science, as exacting as mathematics.

Chapter 14

ECK MORALS AND ETHICS

The chela must be spiritually developed in such a degree that he inspires in those who are the uninitiated a subtle peace of mind and serenity of heart. He must give joy to those around himself; it must radiate from him from within. This is especially true for those Initiates of the Fifth Circle and greater. Dignity and sweet humility are the twin traits in the ECK Chela and this he must not waver from or he'll have physical difficulties as well as difficult human relations. He is ready to go forth to preach the gospel of ECK to the world, revealing ITS secrets to those who are ready to listen. He will show that the MAHANTA is the Divine One who has taken upon himself the human frame for the freedom of Soul.

It has come to my attention that some of the chelas are misusing the ECK, the structure of ECKANKAR, to promote their own wares that they have made themselves or are handling for others, rather than promoting the works of ECK to the world. It is a flagrant violation of the Spiritual Law in ECK to misuse and misrepresent the ECK and ITS principles. An example: This individual had set up an introductory lecture and it was based on ECKANKAR, gave a lecture and it was based on health and then immediately proceeded to promote their products. Another case was where individuals at ECKANKAR seminars were having meetings in their rooms and promoting their products, a tape, some sort of health product or some project that they have going that's special.

The question invariably arises in the study of the

spiritual life: What do morals, values and ethics play? First we must realize that we are here in the lower worlds for the purpose of spiritual experience in all that there is here, including the various forms of negativity. We stimulate the growth of our consciousness by learning from the karmatic effects of our thoughts, words and deeds. The man-made moral codes demand a certain uniformity of behavior which in effect, limits the spectrum of experiences by inhibiting human behavior with various forms of repression. What we must do is go past all morals, past the dichotomy of human extremes, so-called *good* and *evil.*

These illusionary standards are the cause of more sorrow, guilt and anxiety than society can withstand. We must transcend the inhibiting factor of these codes, thus transcending their negative emotions and reach the state of Oneness that emanates from the center of Being.

The Universal Body of the MAHANTA is made up of people of all races, religions and moral fiber. These various people are not obligated to rescind all connections with their traditional values and change to a new set of so-called ECK values, because the only thing recognized as being of any value in ECK is Soul, in the total expansion of consciousness of Soul.

All negative habits and unwholesome modes of behavior will gradually be eliminated by the ECK as each Soul unfolds at his own natural pace, as the little self steps aside in the wake of the Universal Cause. In ECKANKAR the concept of "sin" is meaningless for only when a habit blocks spiritual growth must it be corrected as there are no set "do's" and "don'ts." A chela of ECKANKAR must not waste energy and create further karmatic ties by putting his attention on another individual's limitations and/or seemingly negative behavior, for we are not to judge the experiences of others just as we need the freedom to experience what our own consciousness requires for Soul growth at any particular time. When we do indulge in this type of destructive criticism, we are breaking the ever-expanding circuit of the Master's love.

Man, being a social animal, is one whose very nature implies the necessity of morality in relation to his own existence. We must begin to realize that whatever system of values we use in this earthly life must be an individual thing, established by our own inner authority for the purpose of integrating our inner and outer lives, by setting our own laws and postulates and following them through. By aligning our behavior with the tenets and goals of ECKANKAR, we will be free of the earthly morass of social restriction. This is not situation ethics which implies a versatility of situations, responses to accord with personal satisfaction, but it does include a versatility of response in the sense that, as channels, we may act differently to a given situation according to the level of consciousness of the people involved in the situation, in order that we may reach each respective state of consciousness with the message of ECK.

ECK chelas should not belittle the values of non-ECKists because of the confusion you would cause them if their moral crutches were taken out from under them without giving them the opportunity to stand up on their own, with the inner strength derived from the ECK principles.

Ethics can be defined as that which is not selfish, which is good for the whole, which will not harm one, and will do justice for all concerned, actions for the benefit of all. If we can conform to this principle of obedience to the Universal Law of ECK, all will be well for the individual's free choice, for ourselves and others concerned.

One of the Laws of the ECK and the SUGMAD most of us tend to forget about. As long as we owe one penny to the Earth, or to anyone else, we must return to pay it or work it off in some manner in a form of karma, negative karma. The story of Abraham Lincoln, who walked seven miles to give back a few pennies for overcharging a customer, is an example of how this Law should be respected.

Chapter 15

DEATH: ITS ILLUSIONS

To know one's self, as Socrates put it a few thousand years ago, is really the first commandment of the ECK Masters. It is a great opportunity to make further discoveries in the universe, for lying latent in man's brain is the capacity one million times greater than he is using now. Science has perceived that the average man of today uses only a small percentage of his brain cells.

ECKANKAR, the most ancient religious teaching in all of the universes, has been handed down through time by word of mouth until 1965 when Sri Paul Twitchell began bringing its teaching out into the open through books and discourses. The Living ECK Master of the time and those ECK Masters in the seven Golden Wisdom Temples have taught only to those who were advanced spiritually to the point to be trusted in leaving the physical body temporarily while Soul explored the worlds of this universe including the planets and constellations or the invisible worlds where we go after death of the physical body.

The students in ECKANKAR learn to leave their bodies much in the same way a dying man leaves his shell, except the neophyte does it voluntarily and the process is always under his control, and he can come back into the body at any moment he wishes to return. Otherwise his passing out of the body is practically the same as that of a dying man. He understands what death means and views what lies beyond death. He may even become acquainted with the astral home to which he is to go when he finally takes leave of his physical body.

He may even converse with friends and family who have long before left their physical bodies. This achievement cannot fail to interest the neophyte since it solves the gravest problems of life and destiny. It is one phase of the great work of the Spiritual Travelers in ECKANKAR. They have broken the seal of death and so to them and their charges there is no more death. All of this is positive knowledge, not speculation or guess work. Neither is it the interpretation of any book. It is through experience.

Animals do indeed have a heaven that they go to after translation (death) and there is an ECK Master named Prajapati who takes care of them and guides their spiritual unfoldment. The way into heaven, including the animal heaven, has been taught for ages in ECKANKAR.

The animal form is but one of many forms Soul takes on in a long succession of lifetimes to learn Self-Realization and God-Realization. Animals as well as plants and minerals are divine Soul, only in a different form. Each individual Soul, in whatever form, has four bodies around It: the physical, astral (emotions), the causal (cause and effect and the time track), and the mental. These bodies comprise the microcosm which corresponds with planes in the macrocosm.

Whenever any attempt is made to curb the extinction of an animal species, it is a futile effort, for cycles change and with these changes come the end to a specific animal species. It has served its useful purpose during its stay on this planet and should be allowed to cease functioning in that particular form so that other forms may succeed it.

All living things go through cycles and some species become extinct no matter how man tries to save that species; it will come to its end. The ECKist must not become too emotionally involved in these life cycles and try to change them.

One of the functions of the Living ECK Master is to assist those following the path of ECKANKAR across the borders of death and place them on that plane or place where they have developed themselves spiritually, whether one has just stepped on the path or is even thinking about it.

Cremation is a must for a Master of the Order of Vairagi; however, for the student of ECKANKAR it is not mandatory, simply a matter of choice of the individual. A point for cremation is that there is in many places, a great problem of crowding for the land, an enormous amount of property needed for graveyards, land that could provide food and housing for the living. But the ECKists have that choice for themselves whether they wish to be cremated or buried.

The worry that many people have about death stems from the belief that if the body is not totally destroyed, the Soul may still find Itself tied to it for some time. This is simply not true of the chelas of the ECK Masters, for they are always present at the moment of translation and take care of such things. Any student proficient at Soul Travel makes this change-over so easily that generally no assistance is required. It is nothing more than a natural extension of what he has been doing right along.

The most distinguishing facet of the ECKist's existence is a sense of joy, a joy which arises from his knowledge that death is a myth, that the word *life* has a reality that encompasses states of existence beyond man's imagination, and that the only thing that holds man from the realization of these states is his own self-limiting concepts.

The secret of ECK, in keeping a singing and joyful

heart, is one of the greatest factors of survival in man's life here, as well as the life after what man calls death.

Chapter 16

THE JOYS OF SPIRITUAL GROWTH

There is nothing more important, or real, in this life which man has seen or known until he re-establishes himself in the ECK. This is necessary in order that man might gain God-Realization again without all the ties of the guilt, and control, placed upon man by religion and metaphysics.

Many people or groups without a true spiritual leader have found themselves without hope to gain spiritual unfoldment traveling paths which were claimed to be the authentic way to the heart of God. But how many have learned throughout the centuries that none of these have done much to savor his desires to live in total consciousness of God. This remains a problem within a problem, one for him to solve, yet without any ending as long as he is struggling with the desires and attachments to the material, psychic and mental worlds.

It is very interesting to note that after the chela has spent his first two years studying the teachings of ECK, he finds that it was only the probationary stage which has led him to initiation. This time spent in the ECK classes or in study in private of one's own home can bring him to initiation as well as his time spent in studying the personal discourses in ECK. He is then initiated into the true works of God and he finds the changes of consciousness coming about so many times swifter than he expected.

This is the point in one's spiritual unfoldment at which he begins to experience true reality of the SUGMAD and IT begins to show ITSELF. But only to a few will IT make ITS appearance before this time, for the passing through the various planes of the other worlds constitutes initiations in themselves. The initiate who has taken the second or higher initiations then begins to see that the Dark Night of Soul has passed and he comes into the clear, clean light of God once more. Joy, bliss and happiness replace the negative aspects of the mind and man finds himself able to take up the duties of God without hesitation and with a strength he has never before known. The chela finds, too, that his views of life have changed drastically. He no longer looks at the psychic or material side of life but at the highly spiritual views and the visions of heaven which are now a part of himself. Here it is attitude which brings the success at this point of spiritual growth.

When this change takes place in the chela, he speaks with the positive aspects of God without even thinking of what passes through his mind to be vocalized to the outer world. For it is at this point that the chela does not speak of "my Soul" any longer but now as Soul for he is speaking from the Atma, which is the Soul level. Neither does he think or speak in terms of "the Soul" because he is Soul Itself. When one uses the expression "the or my Soul" he is talking from the body level. Not only does one's language and speech change when he reaches the higher spiritual levels, but he also becomes one who can now speak of "my body or my mind" because he is Soul and speaking from the level of Soul.

As one looks down through the history of ECKANKAR and understands it, one will become aware that whenever the profound teachings of truth of ECK arrived on the human scene, there have been those who gain a partial understanding, then set themselves up as masters. Ego, vanity and a hunger for power drives them on and blinds them to the consequences of their acts. No higher spiritual crime can be committed than to misuse the ECK in order to gain money and power over well-meaning but less aware individuals. There have been various religious groups in different parts of the world that have claimed Paul as a follower or initiated into their line which is not true, and I find today that there are those attempting to claim me as well. I do not have to defend Sri Paul Twitchell or what he wrote, or even ECKANKAR, yet I will stand up and let this body be beaten to a pulp or die for the principles of ECK.

Those groups who have tried to claim any Living ECK Master are false. Once in a while a pseudo teacher makes an attempt to use the ECK to his own ends, but they are largely ignored by the Living ECK Master for he needs to do nothing of himself. The ECK operates swiftly to cleanse Itself of impurities, and the individual who is abusive soon suffers the effects of his own cause.

It is very interesting that, despite man's progress and discoveries, he still remains on the surface of life. For the many thousands of years he has lost the path of ECK but has observed, reflected, recorded what he calls history. Today we have evangelists preaching destruction and Armageddon is near and that you must be saved or you will be destroyed. The only way the impending world disaster is going to be averted is to build more Satsangs and to increase the number of chelas in ECK as vehicles for God. This is for the purpose of having more individual channels for ECK and a greater collective channel for the ECK to have an opportunity to make this world a better place to live and to bring peace to those who want it. There is no other way of doing this. This is also your contribution in helping the

MAHANTA spread the truth and its message of ECK to all concerned. It is also your contribution to mankind. This is the reason that we want ECK Satsangs in every town and city throughout the world. Your contribution of being a vehicle for the ECK Itself makes you important in the works of ECK. It needs you as you need it. The goal is to have several million ECKists around the world by 1985.

It is also very interesting that man, instead of trying to become a vehicle or channel for God, leans on the psychic powers so that he can have personal gain for himself or control of others. This is Lobha, that which is called greed, the third aspect of the five passions of the mind. It is one of the most poisonous of the perversions, and its function is to bind its victim to the material things and cloud the mind to all higher values. When man begins to fall into the psychic trap of this nature, he comes to a stalemate or what is known as the Dark Night of the Soul and lives in this state until his viewpoint is turned outwardly again. Thus he is working for himself personally with the smaller outlook on life instead of trying to do something for the whole or for all life. It isn't exactly working for mankind because this is a negative and limited viewpoint, but he is working for all life—man, beast, insect, plant, mineral—and not only on this planet but every planet and plane throughout the universes of God. The outlook and view of life by the ECKist is not limited by anything. The chela reaches a point in his spiritual unfoldment in ECK where he can see eternity which has no beginning and no ending. It comes out of the path like a long white road stretching up over the hills into the distance, and the ECKist can see all of it with its brilliance and vision that it gives those who have sought it and finally found truth.

Chapter 17

THE IMPORTANCE OF THE ATTITUDE

Countless letters cross my desk from smokers pleading for assistance in overcoming the smoking habit. Sri Paul Twitchell devoted a chapter to this subject in *ECKANKAR: Illuminated Way Letters,* the September 1968 letter on page 117, and again on page 227. Smoking falls under the deadly mind passion called Kama, Lust. A "No Smoking" sign should adorn every ECK meeting no matter where it is held, and should NEVER be permitted at any time before, during or after ECK Satsang classes, Discussion Group meetings, ECK Seminars, ECK functions or activities of any kind. At no time should a chela smoke in the Presence of the Living ECK Master, and if some thought is given to this, remember that the Presence of the MAHANTA is with each and every chela at *all* times once they step upon the path of ECKANKAR. The Master withdraws his Presence from the smoking scene, and Kal, the negative force, presents itself.

When I see that smoking is being permitted during ECK activities, and Arahatas are aware of this, it amazes me. It is very obvious who is being allowed into these meetings...Kal...not ECK! I appreciate hearing from those who are concerned enough to speak up.

If the smoker really wishes to overcome this habit pattern, he must review his attitudes and his goals. As he reaches for that cigarette, is it going to help him gain another step on the ladder to God-Realization? To be a co-worker with the SUGMAD, or a negative habit that binds him to the Kal world? If he is sincere in his desire to overcome smoking or the over-indulgence of food consumption, and calls upon the MAHANTA, the Living ECK Master for assistance in this, he will find it forthcoming with amazing swiftness.

Then I will receive more letters like these: "Don't really know what happened, Master, but suddenly I am free of that nasty horrid cigarette habit. I am pleased for words are inadequate." That person is letting the ECK assist in his daily affairs. Another letter states: "Thank you, thank you, Darwin! Two weeks after I asked for your help, I quit smoking and two weeks yesterday I haven't touched or craved a cigarette. Now maybe I will progress further in my spiritual life." A third writes: "Since stopping smoking last month, my feeling of closeness and awareness of your presence has grown considerably."

All throughout the teachings of ECK, attitude and attention are stressed. As this chela's awareness shows, "At sewing school our teacher said that finishing off our garments on the inside was as important as it had been done on the outside. This brought to my attention the care most of us give our physical appearance on the outside, and how little attention we give to our inside spiritual appearance."

A happy, cheerful attitude is expressed in this note: "An awareness came to me which almost seems too easy to be true. One does not have to travel to the other worlds to be aware of the Here and Now for the understanding of existence. I love seeing God in everyone and everything; it makes me so happy to be alive. I am continually bathing in the Ocean of Love and Mercy. I'm happy to BE."

Two chelas, in letters a day apart, expressed two completely different attitudes in surprisingly similar situations. They had both experienced auto accidents that shook them up and caused considerable damage to their cars. The one exclaimed: "Where is this protection we're supposed to get from the MAHANTA? Why did this inconvenience and this scare happen to me?" The other stated: "I'm so grateful for the Master's constant protection, because I can always repair my car, but it could have been so much worse, and although frightened out of my wits, I wasn't hurt at all."

The chela is tested moment by moment. His attitude throughout the test governs the next step of his unfoldment, the next step on the spiritual ladder. Unless the chela has the stamina for the situations that may beseige him after his initiation, then he will be unable to surrender to the Inner Master and receive the divine teachings.

If the Initiate wishes to escape the creation of any karma of any sort, he must do everything in the name of the Living ECK Master, who acts as his channel to the Divine. As long as this is done, he never creates any new karma, because he is acting solely as the agent of the Master; it is always the principal who is responsible for the acts of his agents. Give all to the Inner Master, obey the commands and reap the rewards. The whole life of the Initiate belongs to the SUGMAD and must be spent in ITS service. When the Initiate does anything, he must have his mind fixed on the Master, and then in love and devotion, he will do the work as a genuine service to the Master and in his name. The Living ECK Master will give in return more than anyone can dream, but it will be done in exchange for the surrender of the chela's self to him. He will gain a freedom that will make him master of spiritual empires and dominant over all things.

Humility and love must take its place in the Initiate and by perfect devotion to the Living ECK Master does he travel into the Supreme Light of

God. In no way is the personal liberty of the Initiate ever interfered with by surrendering to the Inner Master. In fact, he is more free than ever before. The Master is that spiritual transformer by which he can perform miracles for the chela and by which the chela travels into the heavenly worlds. Some chelas feel that "nothing happens" during their spiritual exercises, but this isn't true. They just are not aware of what is taking place in their inner lives.

Should we be looking to the Living ECK Master for anything other than helping us return to God, then we are without a doubt, misunderstanding the whole program of ECK. The Living ECK Master is always guiding the chelas of ECKANKAR, and since he is the representative of the SUGMAD on Earth, then his Will is the Will of the SUGMAD.

Chapter 18

THE AWAKENED CONSCIOUSNESS

In my travels this past year to the various seminars, I have found that a goodly number of Initiates
have difficulty with their spiritual exercises. They
are very simple. Yet for the western man it appears
difficult for some.

Those working from the emotional or astral areas
of consciousness or from the mental field seem to
have the most difficulty. The individual working in
a state of consciousness from the astral or mental
worlds must work at the spiritual exercises on a
regular basis in order to gain the experience and
knowledge of the movement of Soul in order to have
some success in Soul. I have found this to be true of
all circles of initiations. Once one is initiated into a
given circle, he must realize there is a different set of
operating rules to go by for that level of initiation
than the last one. And it's up to the individual to
improve his own ethics at each level of initiation and
not wait for the Living ECK Master to tell him or
her that their ethics need to be improved. The
MAHANTA will let the individual learn their lessons as needed.

An example of this would be the case of a man or
woman and to tell another individual that they are
going to do a certain thing or give their word on a
subject or situation. Like Mary may say to Gus:
"I won't do that anymore," and Mary, say a 6th
Initiate, and Gus is not an Initiate but has certain
principles that he lives by. This couple is married
and Mary breaks her word to Gus. This could be

very upsetting to Gus for he may not say anything the first time, and should it happen a second or third time, soon he'll stop trusting her completely, and the marriage may break up. Or Gus may find some other pretty little girl to be with, to talk to, and just give up on trusting anyone.

Cheating on one's partner is only cheating on one's self. One can never fool the ECK nor the MAHANTA. This is true for all, regardless whether one is married or not. The people you work with or for, your word must be your bond as one grows in their knowledge of the ECK. One could meet a total stranger and agree to help him in some way, then at the last minute decide not to go through with the commitment. Again the Living ECK Master is there as the Inner Master and knows you've only held yourself back from the next step at that moment of time. Sure, there's always another chance and you must work back to that chance, and work for it. It requires not only love which is limited in the dual worlds, but devotion, respect, honesty and loyalty. However, it may be your job or your marriage, even a possible marriage that is blown to the wind, and this is what really goes to the heart.

I've found in my travels that there's an enormous lack of respect for each other as Initiates in ECK, for the works in ECK in some degree by some. Like *The Mystic World* is for the Initiate only and not for the rest of the world. The material that is in there I find many do not read, such as some of the special notices, etc. And they're missing a lot of what's going on. Especially if they're going to be an active physical vehicle for God.

The *ECK World News* is a different sort of publication. That particular paper I get extra copies. I'll put them on a plane, in a dentist's office, a doctor's office. I'll leave it in a library, to name a few places.

It's endless how it reaches various individuals. It's an uplifting, positive paper or magazine, however you want to look at it. There is not another publication like it in the world. Sure, it might be slanted slightly, but it's telling the ECKist's side and point of view. Their stories, and that's what it wants to be. Just as the *ECK Mata Journal.* These are stories of the ECKists and from and by the ECKists, not for the ECKists but for the rest of the world. Yet they are uplifting to the rest of the ECKists as well.

Another area that I found in my travels this past year in going through various areas and talking with various people and listening, I have found that an enormous number of individuals are more interested in their material survival than their spiritual, and gaining the knowledge of the heavenly worlds. *The Shariyat-Ki-Sugmad* points this out that if you seek and gain the knowledge of God, all the things of the world are added to you. If the survival of man in this world is to come about, then he must find time for creative activity in the spiritual works of ECK. Until this happens within the individual or the group he's in, the Satsang group, etc., to do something of a spiritual nature besides subsist in the materialistic world, there is little opportunity, for excessive time spent in contemplation, meditation or prayer does not automatically produce spiritual results.

If one looks about oneself, he'll find that most of the people are preoccupied in their waking state for the comforts and for survival as long as possible in any state that gives him joy, regardless whether a mystical state or a materialistic state for comfort, he lives through periods of skepticism and drops it when the comfort states are leaving him.

When such states of comfort are regained, he once more establishes himself in the persistent ideal of ease and happiness with his materiality. He knows, lives and is aware of life in the part of his physical and human senses. Other than this, there is little else in life for him. One gains material possessions and gives life the least he can, but always in hopes that it will return him greater rewards.

There's a statement in *The Shariyat-Ki-Sugmad*, Book One, Chapter II, that Sri Paul Twitchell brought forth from the Golden Wisdom Temples, in which I wish to quote three small paragraphs:

"ECK is the embodiment of all attributes of life, of spiritual enlightenment, of vitality and vibrancy. IT is endowed with vibrancy. IT is endowed with intelligence as opposed to Jad, or materialism, and is the principle which finds expression in the word Chaitanya, which in Sanskrit embraces all things noted here.

"The ECK descends and ascends in vibratory currents, producing music inherent and inborn that gives joy to the heart of those who have the power to hear ITS melody. The middle aspect of ECK is light and ITS lower aspect is intelligence. IT vibrates and reverberates through all worlds. Within the higher worlds IT creates the sound, the music of life; within the psychic worlds IT creates light and in the worlds of matter IT creates intelligence.

"All in all, IT creates, sustains and gives freedom to that chela who is able to hear the music of the SUGMAD, to see the light of the worlds and to know with the intellect. With this comes freedom, the liberation that brings to Soul the very essence of happiness. This is the true freedom, the true happiness, the true knowledge of God."

Contemplate on the above, for in ECKANKAR, the Path of ECK, as one goes beyond the dual worlds, one comes into the understanding that the word that the Eastern religious thought and those who understand the word Chaitanya, which in Sanskrit means "embraces all things," is speaking of the Universal Mind. It is part of the ECK stream but it is that part that dwells within the dual worlds, as a lesser light which Kal uses. And getting beyond that thirst for materialism which is one of the five passions of the mind that one must watch daily and constantly and not get caught up in it.

The ECKist who reaches the true spiritual stages beyond the level of phenomena becomes intoxicated with visions of the true reality and he no longer cares for the conventional form. He grows beyond property, religion, philosophy, economics, and other materialistic forms which are suffocating to him. He can have the materialistic things but becomes unattached. The rest of the world, the uninitiated, don't know what to think of this type of person. For the ECKist who has had intense prolonged experiences finds it very difficult to communicate to those who are the uninitiated. Life as it is in the materialist worlds sadly rejects the experiences of the ECKists and the validity of the Living ECK Master.

Chapter 19

GAINING THE KNOWLEDGE OF GOD

How you live your life is up to you. Don't let others tell you how to live your life, whether it is a neighbor or a friend. I do not tell others even though I know the ECKist's deepest secrets.

ECKANKAR and those in ECK have nothing to do with politics in our society and trying to change society and the ways of man. It is an individual freedom, complete freedom for the individual and that means survival throughout eternity. This means knowing who you are and knowing that you are taken care of.

Shifting the states of consciousness to higher states takes a long time for we need to drop certain things which we have been taught from childhood to adulthood. This shifting of states of consciousness, through the expansion of consciousness, which takes the individual's own initiative, is very simple and very easy, yet it is very hard until you learn. But for that person, whether he is out with a broom cleaning streets or behind a desk shuffling papers, does not have to put his attention onto the SUGMAD (God) at all times because the ECK, or that which sustains all of us and all life, is constantly flowing through us. If the individual realizes that, he can go about his daily duties or responsibilities for his family without dropping his job or wanting to run off to the hills to some part of the world and search for a greater understanding.

There are no crosses in ECKANKAR, whatsoever, to bear, but one gains and understands his responsibility to himself and to that we know as

God or SUGMAD. The rest of the world isn't aware of ECKANKAR although some of them are enlightened in practicing the various principles of ECK. However, they are not really aware of that which can take one into totality or total awareness.

For all of the problems that exist in today's world such as you see around you (there have been wars and all kinds of things happening), when such a positive force as the ECK comes into a city, county, or state, things happen. People and areas have been controlled by various thought forms and patterns and a change has to come about. It must change in order for man to survive, not only during this life time.

If we can let individuals know that there is a way to rise above the problems at hand in a state of consciousness and not be affected emotionally, then the perspective and perception that is developed by the individual, subjectively and objectively, can lead him into a much richer and fuller life and without the factor of guilt that is impressed, not only by the ways of society and man's religion, but the materialistic world.

It takes thought first for that individual who learns how to get beyond himself objectively or subjectively. I think it was Yaubl Sacabi, the ECK Master, that spoke of one way which is to purify the mind and to live in purity which is really the first requirement for us as human beings and being able to go beyond ourselves. Once an individual learns this, he is not going to go back to many of his old ways of thought or of doing things.

Without the vehicle of thought it would be impossible to do Soul Travel. Where the problem comes with those who climb the spiritual ladder and gain a little understanding of themselves and the Far Country, is that individual can cut off the current which is given to them through the initiation. They will either know or they won't, depending on their awareness, that when the current shuts off, when the vehicle is closed to the expression of God through them, that something has happened.

The Masonic Order had the secret word and lost it. It was given to them. Of course, Initiates of ECKANKAR are given certain secrets of the Far Country and they are observed as to how they handle that themselves, how they perform.

Some individuals have expressed a desire to get back into the area they were before and wondered why it was cut off and how they could get back to that point on the spiritual ladder where they could soar in the Sound Current or have that moment of bliss. One of the ways is that one can feel this essence of God which is spoken of as ECK. It will flow through the body and down throughout the legs and in the hands and arms. When this starts with many people, the individual tries to direct it. The moment this takes place in the form of thought, it is cut off. I am speaking of the current. It is reduced back to that which you had before you stepped on the path of ECKANKAR.

By being a vehicle and letting It go without directing It, by taking care of our responsibilities as we know how, and living within the laws, whether they are those established by our courts or the spiritual laws, that one learns and can keep from cutting off the flow.

Many claim to be a vehicle for one of the ECK Masters. This will close off that current perhaps swifter than any other way because none of the ECK Masters work through any of the individuals, whether they are ECKists or any other human being. We have nothing to do with mediumship. We partake of nothing that is known as spiritualism.

By chanting the many names of God you are able to purify thought and the mind. Then you will find that living in the physical world takes on a completely different feeling for you.

It is up to the individual how he uses not only the knowledge but the ability to perform things for himself as well as others, for the good of the whole. Whether the individual is at work, at play or on a busy street, if he needs to rise above what is happening, if he is being brought down in a state of consciousness or feels very negative, that individual at that point of time can rise above that.

When one has this ability to rise above time, space, energy and matter, or to the Soul plane, you can look down to the lower planes that exist, the etheric, the mental, the causal, the astral, and the physical. All knowledge is at your disposal.

I don't have to prove anything to anyone. The individual can prove it to himself. I attend each Satsang class regardless of what part of the world it is in. There are witnesses to that. This is one of the functions of the Living ECK Master and at that time there might be other ECK Masters there also. I will either be at home writing, reading, or performing some other duty and consciously be aware of what is taking place. I don't prove it nor does ECKANKAR have to be proven to anyone because the individual can prove it to himself.

The knowledge that exists for the individual is enormous but very few partake of it and it is very simple to partake of it. This is knowledge that man has not recorded yet in his history books or literature. The teaching itself is a secret teaching. Through the ECK books and ECK discourses you will find there is material that does not appear anywhere else on this planet, yet that is just a start.

The greater teaching to the individual on this path is given in the dream state or he is taken out at night to a Wisdom Temple of which there are seven, three in the physical and one on each succeeding plane. This is where the great teaching takes place, the secret part of it.

When I was learning to be an adept at this and go beyond myself, I had heard that all of man's basic philosophy and the basic scriptures (not that which the saints or the disciples wrote but just the basic text) derived from a set of books, The Shariyat-Ki-Sugmad. They are in these Wisdom Temples. I was shown and able to read them. But here again, I cannot prove it to anyone, but the individual can prove it to himself.

When one reaches the pure positive God-Consciousness state, we do not become one with God as other paths teach. They would become an atom structure within God while we retain our individuality throughout eternity.

My only concern is helping those out of this low vibration who want to know more about themselves, not only in this world but also in the higher worlds and be able to have an experience while they are here.

No one from the past died to serve you. Death is an illusion not fully understood. On the other side of the world of illusion there is true reality. Youth, pressured adults, as the tempo of living goes up, may commit suicide. ECK can be a disruptive force, but always peaceful and loving. We need those idle moments of silence to rise above the physical consciousness. There are three main things to consider in developing the vehicle of ECK: faith, devotion and responsibility.

It seems that there is quite a bit of conversation today in different circles about death. Psychologists and many of our educators are attempting to unshackle many of the old ways of thought that have been impressed upon man through fables, coming not only from religions, but from various thinkers. The treasures of heaven are NOW and not tomorrow.

In October 1965 quite a change took place, not only on this planet but throughout the universe and all universes, when the Rod of Power of the ECK Mastership was passed from Rebazar Tarzs to Peddar Zaskq. It occurred again in October 1971 when the Rod of Power was passed to Dap Ren (Sri Darwin Gross).

When you go through life, regardless of what sort of battle or circumstances you encounter, you have a tool that is far greater than the modern tools of technology and far subtler than anything known to man. This adeptness, which is necessary to grow into and unfold, requires the expansion of consciousness through the initiative of the individual. There are many that think that this can be forced through certain tortures to the body. This happens in the East, though some of it is starting to be carried over to the West. It is not necessary, neither does it require some secret potion or drug. It takes a little self-discipline.

Some of you in looking back to 1965 and prior to 1965 may remember that the tempo was pretty high. There was a lot of spiritual unrest in the United States and throughout the world. It is starting to pick up again so remember that when the emptiness comes within or without, the only way you can fill yourself full of love to crowd out the darkness is if you can contemplate on the love of the SUGMAD during your contemplative exercises.

The movement of ECKANKAR is not here to sway man's thinking. It is an individual path. You have the choice as to how to rule and direct your universe and world without affecting those around you in a negative sense.

Now each of you can derive different aspects of the teachings of ECK which can be heard as Sound and seen as Light and gain the knowledge and wisdom that is yours for the taking. But always remember—are you ready for the next step? Because you might not be prepared for what comes with it. Ask the Inner Master for the guidance for that unfoldment. Do not be afraid to ask the question.

In this material world, there is no perfection as we think of perfection. The only perfection that can be reached is in the Soul body and through Its development into the pure, positive God Worlds. And if the line isn't too straight, take a look at it from another angle. There's a reason for that. To observe an object, a situation, a point that disturbs you within yourself, that upsets you or you mentally haggle over it, look at it from over here or back there. Because from up there it looks different than from down here. And if you look at these aspects that trouble you, the questions that arise within yourself as ends from the points of view and develop this to a daily use, you will find that the area of conscious expansion of consciousness becomes unlimited. Then you start to realize that it exists all around and about you, permeates all things and sustains all life, and you become a greater channel and vehicle for IT, this thing called ECK.

Chapter 20

FALSE TEACHERS

They speak in the voices of the false prophets, pseudo-masters; they bring about the obstacles and troubles to the mind and flesh of the spiritual seekers. They interfere with our plans and raise their voices to drown out any of those seeking truth of the works of ECK. They will falsely represent themselves as the teachers and masters of ECKANKAR and will use those who are the simple, guideless and naive to listen to the voices of the false teachers, the masters who claim they are teaching ECKANKAR.

These entities, these false prophets and pseudo-masters who lay claim to being the ECK Master, or who teach another faith with the title of the spiritual master, are simply the co-workers of the Kal Niranjan. They live and exist in the psychic world only and cannot give true spiritual liberation to a Soul, yet, they make claims that their works are worthy of the greatest tasks. The ECK works are the most powerful in this world and the MAHANTA, the Living ECK Master, is the most powerful vehicle for the ECK.

It is unfortunate in these times that people instead of believing in the works of ECK, run after the teachings of the orthodox and the false, even without any visible evidence in their favor. The Kal has so cleverly designed this world that people easily believe what suits their purpose, but they will not believe the MAHANTA, the Living ECK Master, who tries to present truth to all in the best possible manner, but demand miracles of him. This shows they are the victim of the Kal, because they believe what his followers say without evidence, while they demand miracles of the MAHANTA.

As said in *The Shariyat-Ki-Sugmad*, the Living ECK Master strives constantly to take the chela out of the earthly gains level, but he never makes rules nor rituals, never lays down laws and proclaims his way to God as the better way, although it is. He knows that all religions are pseudo and in the minority, but he never states this in any of his works. He never asks that anyone follow his path and abide by his own conduct and words. He knows that many men cannot do this as they have established their own consciousness in religion and will be offended should he demand they follow him.

All religions are for the benefit of the leader with exception of the Path of ECKANKAR. The Living ECK Master teaches all who will listen to his word that this is truth and the chela must learn to separate truth from false teachings. Until man has learned to do this he is apt to wander about this world of mind and body through centuries of reincarnations.

The Christian Bible refers to the wheels of transmigration, reincarnation, in the following references:

Hebrews . . . . Chapter 9, Verse 27
Malachi . . . . Chapter 4, Verses 5, 6
Ezekiel . . . . Chapter 16, Verses 48 thru 55
Ezekiel . . . . Chapter 37, Verses 1 thru 14
Ecclesiastes . . . . Chapter 1, Verses 9 thru 11
Ecclesiastes . . . . Chapter 3, Verses 15 thru 21
Matthew . . . . Chapter 11, Verses 12 thru 15
Matthew . . . . Chapter 17, Verses 10 thru 13
1 Peter . . . . Chapter 3, Verses 19, 20
1 Peter . . . . Chapter 4, Verse 6

No one can escape the round of birth and death by

following the pseudo teachers and masters, or even the Kal, the lord of the realm, who is the founder of the orthodox religion in the lower worlds; yet, he himself cannot go beyond the cycle of transmigration. This is true, especially in present times when the majority of pseudo teachers are merely educated men, not true teachers or masters. For one never finds a real master until he reaches the MAHANTA, the Living ECK Master.

The spiritual community of ECK is in the hearts of all those following ECK. It is here that they can communicate with one another over vast distances and can bring love, wisdom, and happiness with each other. No other followers of any master, teacher, occult or religious teaching can do this. It is just the privilege of the ECKists to be able to communicate with the MAHANTA, the Living ECK Master, in his subtle form and with one another in their own set of bodies. This is the defeat of the Kal and that which brings about the tremendous love and understanding that each ECKist has for the MAHANTA, the Living ECK Master, and for one another.

Many profess faith in ECK outwardly, but have not given up their longing for materiality in their hearts. This lack of faith is due to their ignorance of the spiritual works of ECK. Often they do not take the pains to read or study properly, nor do they listen to the MAHANTA. They criticize and harp upon their own pains and troubles, often blaming the Living ECK Master and in their ignorance, do not understand that this is a dangerous practice. Everything they say against the MAHANTA and the ECK will return to take from them. Their losses are due to their own thoughts and actions.

It is the works of the Kal to use religions, ministers and lay persons to bring about the downfall of the ECK because IT is truth. There will be those who call themselves ECK Masters and disguise themselves under the robe of the ECK, but they are prophets with false faces who are deceiving to take in the ECKists, but few, if any, who are truly followers of the ECK are ever deceived by these agents of the Kal.

In order to break the hold that a problem may have on the mind of a chela, the MAHANTA frequently assists the chela to try to solve a false problem unknowingly, by acting consistently upon it. This often releases the chela, who suddenly sees through any problems of his own and finds liberation. However, the religions, the occult groups, transcendental meditation, etc., feel that the state of liberation that they may enter into is the Cosmic Consciousness or Christ-Consciousness. This is not true. For the ECKist, once released, goes into a much higher state than this.

The mysteries of speech, sight and hearing in the physical world are, indeed, strange. The MAHANTA speaks only through the inner channels and never outward to his chela except in the physical flesh or by missives. When he instructs, it is often on the inner channels or by the written word. Sometimes entities even attempt to change the written word in these letters or personal instructions the MAHANTA might send to his chelas. It is not often done, but these entities of the Kal Niranjan are always seeking opportunities to do harm to the chelas in order to get them away from the ECK, which is to their discredit. They are always promising something greater to the chelas in order to lure them away from the path of ECK, but there is nothing comparable to this ECK way of life.

Chapter 21

THE ILLUSIONS OF LIFE

If the average modern man is asked what he is living for, and what is the aim of his striving, he will probably tell you, with some embarrassment, that he lives "to enjoy life," "to support his family," "to have fun," "to make money," or "to achieve something meaningful and worthwhile." But in reality, we are all aware that no one seems to know exactly what he is living for. If he broods over the things that surround him and the kind of world he is living in, he will soon become skeptical about the relevance of raising these questions. He cannot help but ask honestly, "Can we really know the right answers, do we have any choice over these matters, and after all, what difference will it make?"

In spite of the unavoidable resignation and bewilderment that the modern man feels, sooner or later he finds himself compelled to choose between two alternatives: he can either turn to religion with blind faith and hope, or turn to the world and "make the best of it." It is certain that men choose the former, not always because they are convinced of the truth of religion, but rather because doubt and despair have made their lives unbearable. On the other hand, they choose the latter, not because they have proven the untruth of religion, but because, in all likelihood, their spirits are deadened by pessimism and indifference. One fact, however, remains clear: in both cases, the choice is made under the coercion of pain, sorrow or despair.

The majority of modern men are deprived of the opportunity and privileges of leading a rich spiritual life as their forefathers once did.

Is it really advantageous to lead a life without any suffering? Many believe that misfortune and grief are prerequisites for spiritual awakening.

Is it not true that science and technology at their best, can alleviate but not eliminate the sufferings of men?

It appears that events change, but what really happens is that we shift our viewpoint from event to event, even though the event is stationary and fixed. All creation is finished. All events, all situations and all forms are co-existing and make themselves known in our lives as we view them. It is the recognition of them which is important, the awakening of man. Man does not evolve, he awakens. He moves in his assumptions of his own limited consciousness.

Nothing is ever to be created, it is only manifested. What is called creativity is only that process of becoming aware of what already is. You simply become aware of increasing portions of that which already exists.

The God we know in ECK is like a great whirling vortex, out of which comes Spirit. This Spirit is like a sea, and man is a fish swimming in this sea. This is what we call the Ocean of Love and Mercy.

When the world of man is illuminated, he becomes a part of God, the realization of the Absolute. Illumination comes through waiting upon the Lord; that is, by resting in the consciousness of the Omnipresence. It is not through struggle, effort, supplication or merit. No one except those who are traveling the path of ECK can determine when it occurs.

The type of mind that grasps the illuminated state, is one with randomness. A mind which can change under any circumstance. The higher a Soul travels the spiritual path of ECK, the less Its burdens become, and the easier it is to change swiftly from one course to another.

God never established an exclusive group for the liberation of man. He has given the power to many for the portal or way back to his kingdom. There are certain paths that one must follow, some better than others, because men are at all sorts of levels of consciousness and not all can follow the one universal way called ECK.

Each man's world is a solid thought or materialized mind stuff. The idea is to bring into expression the good and beautiful. This is done by getting the good and beautiful properly arranged in the consciousness.

Here is the most important part of life's message in ECK: it is not what we do that determines our experience in life, but it is what we expect. Even if you have done all the correct things, and still maintain the haunting fear that things will go wrong, they will go wrong. Is it because you are bad, sinful, or evil? No. It is because you have the belief.

With the above understood, we are coming into the level of understanding in ECK wherein we cease trying to demonstrate things but, rather, move into a greater expression and find that the things we need are already supplied, we demonstrate the giver and not the gift! We demonstrate God and not the things of God.

Saints, devils, and credulous fools are made of the same identical stuff. They all have visions. They see the same truth from different aspects. Devils exploit stupidity. They create blinding fear that gives them power over others. Such fear inflates the devil's feeling of importance, and it makes the fools think that the devils are the only safe leaders to follow. But the visions of the saints like prisms letting light into darkness diffuses the material fog,

112

the fog that blinds the best men and makes men victims of want, disease, and crime. The visions of the saints let in affluence and magnanimity and vigor. Naturally, the devils hate this. If they can't pervert the saint's vision to their own ends, they try to destroy it.

One of the most prevalent misunderstandings is that the Law of God works only for those who have a devout or religious objective. This is a fallacy. It works just as impersonally as the law of electricity works. It can be used for greed or selfish purposes as well as for noble tasks. But it should always be borne in mind that ignoble thoughts and actions inevitably result in unhappy consequences.

The secret of harmonious love is the development of the spiritual consciousness, as any spiritual traveler in ECK will tell you. In this consciousness, fear and anxiety disappear and life becomes meaningful, with fulfillment as its keynote. The individual becomes a dweller in the higher consciousness.

This is one of the differences that ECK makes with established religion. The authorities put a great deal of emphasis on rituals, moral codes, and laws, but seldom do they speak about rising above good and evil, or love and hate, or polarizing upon the dichotomy of good. This is one of the most subtle points of all life. Remember James 1:8: "A double-minded man is unstable in all his ways."

For the non-academic student wants simply to practice and experience a way of overcoming the hang ups (klesa) which follow from the illusion that one is, in fact, an individual ego, separate from the external and inconceivable ground of all existence.

Man has put the eastern teachers and Jesus Christ on pedestals of reverence so high that he is automatically excluded from the higher states of consciousness.

Man may have potentialities of all kinds for the psychotechnology of clairvoyance, telekinesis, precognition and telepathy (not to mention epipathy, catapathy, apopathy, and peripathy). Power-games of this kind are not, however, the main concern of the ECKist. On the contrary, the point is to realize that by virtue of what you always are, have been, and will be, there is no need whatsoever to *prove* yourself.

There are three kinds of individuals: those whose intelligence is completely dull; those whose intelligence is of average quality, able to understand some truths which are especially evident; those endowed with an intelligence better equipped for acute perceptions, who are fit to penetrate below and beyond the surface of the world of physical phenomena and grasp the causes which are at work there.

It is enough to direct the attention to those last, to say to them: "Look from this point of view, consider that" and they perceive what is to be perceived there where they have been told to look; they understand what is really the thing which one has pointed out to them.

The teachings of ECK are secret, they will remain 'secret' for the individuals who will hear what is said to them, and will grasp nothing of it but the sound.

It is the Living ECK Master that the 'secret' depends on. The ECK Master can only be he who opens the door: it is for the disciple to be capable of seeing what lies beyond. It is thus that the day's teachings, transmitted orally from the ECK Master to disciple for many generations, have been passed on and preserved from oblivion. You have heard them. Do with them as you think fit. They are simple, but, like a powerful battering ram they run

114

counter to the wall of false ideas rooted in the mind of man and the emotions which delight him, casting him into suffering...try!

Chapter 22

PRAYER: HELPFUL OR HARMFUL?

I am increasingly concerned with the matter of prayer in the public schools, in government and any other secular institutions.

There are two points of view about prayer. One is that it is absolutely useless and what will be, will be. Those who feel this way are generally indifferent as to whether or not it is done publicly.

The other point of view, and it is mine also, is that prayer is an effective way, if done with enough intensity, to influence the directions of events, or influence the conscience of another.

Often those who believe sincerely in the power of prayer are naive about the dynamics of it and what they are doing. It is, in truth, thought power, and when used to influence the direction of events or humans without their request or permission, it is no less than an invasion of that individual's sanctity.

Whatever one's point of view is about prayer, I feel that every individual who is in a position of responsibility concerning legislation on this subject should be as aware of the spiritual laws, of non-interference with another's BEINGNESS as they are of the constitutional laws regarding rights.

If a person wishes to meditate, contemplate or pray, they should. Whenever I can I grab 15 or 20 minutes, or at least a half an hour once a day. It's best if one can take half an hour out of the 24-hour period sometime. This will usually carry the person through the 24-hour period. Everything goes in cycles and this is one way to assist one through some of the rough parts of the day. I help only those

116

who make a request though. To help another person who hasn't requested it and who may not be ready for that next step would be interfering with his consciousness.

To pray for anyone without asking their permission is a violation of spiritual law. It's an occult form of black magic. In addition, communes and ashrams of the sort that were in Guyana (December 1978) violate the laws of Spirit (ECK). Individuals who attempt to do this sort of thing are going to have a lot of problems and difficulties due to the negative forces inherent in the human consciousness. It causes a breakdown in the spiritual, ethical and moral structure. Because there is a reliance on the group's consciousness in a communal situation, there is a false feeling of strength that can be swept away suddenly. True spiritual strength can only be gained by going to that temple within oneself with the guidance of the Living ECK Master.

When prayer is used by someone in great authority or in the hands of a ruthless person, great results may occur but always the penalty must be paid by the user of such power. Religious history is full of anecdotes praising the use of saintly power but it is a violation of a spiritual law to move another person for any purpose without their permission. It is one of the practices of the clergy to change the consciousness of the nonconformist so he cannot harm the cause of the church.

This is also true of the mass media today. They disobey the law of God daily by newspapers, TV, radio, magazines and books, purposely influencing the reader or the viewer through slanted material. Even advertising is a form of an occult technique to influence the buyer to buy a certain product whether the buyer wants it or not.

God knows all that goes on in ITS worlds, the

universes created for one's experiences and unfoldment, yet IT never interferes with the freedom of man's individual consciousness. Since this is true of the Creator, man does not have the right to interfere with another's decisions or thoughts.

Some people claim that it is the "will of God" that this or that occur, trying to change others' minds to accept their ideas and goals, but this is the method used by a sly person, or perhaps an ignorant one, who is the tool of a power play.

An example: the more religious groups pray for those wallowing in sin, the more crime and corruption will exist.

Many are teaching the masses to love everyone, to love their neighbors, and that's fine, if it's with a detached love. If someone tries to give you something, make sure there are no strings attached. It is great to receive and to give, always greater to give, but it's just like giving a part of your heart in a sense of love. You have to be very careful who you give love to for many times it backfires. It is better to give goodwill rather than say, "Brother, I love you," because what he is going to do with that love may well interfere with that person's state of consciousness. Give of goodwill toward another without trying to change his consciousness, or his conscience.

We cannot go around telling people what they should or should not have, whether it involves prayer or not. Orthodox religions taught that to beg, seek and ask of the Divine Deity would bring about answers to problems and questions, supply them with material needs and work out their difficult situations for them, but when these petitions to God did not bring forth answers, many would give up and never even try again.

In order to gain something from the invisible

worlds we must be at a certain spiritual level in life. If we are below that level of receiving it never shall be ours. We receive exactly according to the spiritual development gained. In order to receive anything from God we must be open to accepting that which we request.

Prayer and the ritual of petition was used by the clergy as a mysterious, secret sort of approach to God. It only enmeshed the untrained individual deeper and deeper into the realm of karma. When one uses mental prayer to get rid of a spouse or obtaining money, others might be involved that the person had not counted on and thus the karmic web widens further.

Too many of us want life to do something for us. We beseech God to give us spiritual things, material goods, and when our prayers go amiss we turn to another way that seems to offer more in the way of miracles.

When we come to the realization that Spirit is the underlying cause of all effect, we find we cannot be dependent upon any person or thing, only the ECK (Spirit). By use of this inner power, after it has been developed through the guidance and protection of the Living ECK Master, our lives will be shaped and manifested through our states of consciousness into the outer world.

We do not use denials, affirmations, prayer, rituals nor any of the many other forms of outer discipline. None of these can help us. Tradition, habit, customs, environment and heredity will imprison anyone, leaving one unable to work on the disciplination of the inner self, the discipline not of the mental realms but that of emotion and imagination.

Prayer is a visualizing, a seeing in the mind's eye of something that is desired. When prayer is used for others, he must be linked to the one prayed for by faith and both linked to the outflow of Divine Spirit. Open your heart to all in true loving kindness and into the heart will flow the added blessings of Spirit.

Chapter 23

THE ATTITUDES OF ECKANKAR

Those that live to themselves existing in the bliss of God alone cannot do so for long for they will come to the unbalancing of their minds and bodies. While in this body serving out a duty upon earth whether we be a Master or a common laborer, we must balance the spiritual forces between ourselves and all other things be it a tree, a house, a dog, a human being, or the rose in the garden.

One might ask what this has to do with the spiritual traveler being sufficient unto himself? Can he dwell in the cosmic consciousness whenever he desires? Or is this a belief of man based upon false knowledge?

You might say simply this: In the material world we need the good fellowship of every individual to exist, but if we have the love of each individual with whom we are in relationship daily then the inner powers are lifted and a channel of love is open to SUGMAD through and by the efforts of others.

The ECK Masters refuse to consider themselves as intermediaries between the divine, the universal mind, and man. The Spiritual Travelers in ECKANKAR are the agents of God, but they will not allow themselves to be used for anyone to rely upon them as a support; this includes the Living ECK Master of the time. The individual can lean upon him momentarily, but the purpose is to teach every man to take his own responsibility and stand upon his spiritual feet anywhere at any time.

The attitude of ECKANKAR is the very independence of Soul. Therefore, we must cease to cherish opinions of others, the things of this world, and thoughts. The essence, nature, of ECK is hence freedom from all things, not only the attachment to an idea as a factor that conditions the mind and holds Soul in bondage to it, but the simple preference for one idea over another or one opinion over another and for value of one thing or idea rather than the other. All equally enslave Soul to mind, thus chaining the divine, if possible, to the lower aspects of God.

Soul is the central reality of the individual. Soul of Itself dwells in the ultimate cosmic consciousness, God-realization, at all times unless of course mind gets too strong and becomes wild and tries to pull It down to the lower levels of the universe. This is hardly possible for when this happens Soul withdraws and leaves mind to run the body which it will do, but to the detriment of the physical body. Soul being a happy entity will not be controlled by any thing other than the ECK, the holy spirit. Thus we must devote ourselves to the practical work of our daily lives and try to realize the guidance of ECK in every affair. This depends on the nonattached attitude in the realization of doing everything for the universal or the totality of SUGMAD. What many ECKists do not realize is that the moment that we start creating special points, ideas, distinctions, we exile ourselves from the state of God Consciousness and miss the infinite freedom of reality actually underlining the teachings of ECK. We can see that the illuminated way to God does not have any difficulties except that it refuses to become attached to any preferences.

That old saying that there's a hairline difference between heaven and earth is very true. When one realizes this then we become more aware that an absence of dogma exists. And it is only when we are seeking anything other than God and living in the area of rituals and dogmas that we suffer from the desires that are unworthy.

Since freedom of Soul is to be had here and now, all we must do is to recognize and live in the assumption of our knowledge. We must feel the extraordinary sensitivity and delicacy of our relationship with the sense of freedom. But this will bring up questions from dogmatic thinkers, when speaking of freedom of Soul, who will not admit to the possibility of the fundamental freedom and a non-conditioned mind. The skeptic will defend his particular views and beliefs with arguments with which he identifies himself. He wants his own personal ideological preferences to triumph. But here is the point—We have nothing to defend, for we have no personal idea on anything. We possess nothing. Therefore we have no reason to fight, for wisdom consists in not treasuring opinions.

This philosophy of nothingness is not a pretense on the part of the Spiritual Travelers. They are aware that pure freedom is never conceived, it lives, but only becomes alive when all concepts cease. The ECKists do not revolt against dogma and beliefs, and should one revolt then he is adding a lot of trouble not only to the present but perhaps to the future moments of time, weeks, or months. But the ECKists allow Soul to become the impersonal channel of the ECK which uses It as the means to uplift the world of matter, then we become the pole of the God power to change the Consciousness of all with whom we come into contact.

We know the difference between being awake and sleeping, between light and darkness, freedom and slavery. There can be no halfway for the traveler. The passage from one state to the other constitutes a spiritual transmutation, hence there is an essential change or a sudden change in one who has experienced true God-Realization and the liberation of Soul. When the mind gives up its inner tension the God-Realization is often sudden, unexpected, and spontaneous. This experience of light and sound comes pouring into Soul like a burst of thunder and lightning. It lifts us into the heights of the true kingdom and snaps us out of the sleep state into the consciousness of awareness. We are now alive and at once become the true channel of Truth. The whole secret of our power lies not in the fact that we have the secret of power, but of life itself. It must be understood that the difficulty or the problem of the Saints within organized religion lies in the thought that once they had reached the formless, that of the true kingdom of heaven, they began to make the mistake of putting themselves into the limitations of symbols and cherished opinions. All experiences of the mystics within religions down through the past have done this and find themselves limited by the mind which intervenes and creates tragic anxiety within the symbols of the adored formless vision and sounds. Therefore in spite of their lofty thoughts, they were able to penetrate only the limits of the mental plane where we find symbols, ideas, and forms existing. So many times their mystic's emotion is often the result of simple transmutation of the body energies to the mental plane and have the physical sensationalism accompanied by a psychic experience. The Spiritual Traveler does not need discipline nor is his realization of the spiritual self of an emotional or mental nature. He transcends beyond the mind and definitely frees himself from identification with the body, the mind, and thought. This is the state which we are seeking, the place in the ultimate realm of heaven, that we are living in now and it takes only self recognition to assure us of this state. All can dwell in the consciousness of the SUGMAD here and now.

Chapter 24

MAN'S IMAGE OF GOD

In my recent trip to the East, particularly India and Kashmir, I have learned that there is quite a difference in the religious beliefs in that part of the world. The same beliefs are not shared by lamas and yogis. The yogi cannot believe that the teachings of any one man can be final. He sees that every human being has access to all knowledge right within himself. Now this is true up to a point but they do not go beyond the Void and it takes the Living ECK Master whose Atma is lit in order to take the followers of ECK or anyone through that dark Void into the pure positive God Worlds. They must step on the path of ECKANKAR in order to attain it, while the lamas are enhanced to enlightenment of Buddha alone. In all probability each human being will unfold in their thought and realize their mightiness. A Christian will reach the Christ-consciousness, a Buddhist will reach the Buddha-attainment and so on. All have their god and on every hand one can hear that God made man in his image. That image that's spoken of that God made as man was derived from the ECK Masters that have been able to appear to man. All nations and all peoples have their different gods.

Some have their god of fire, others a god of harvest, etc. Each stresses the fact that their god is better than his fellow man. To the individual that is seeking a spiritual understanding I can see how they get so mixed up and reach a state of neurosis when they study more than one path at a time, for I can understand that God made man in his image but they don't know what image the scriptures are speaking of.

For IT, God that is, when visited in ITS entirety is pure energy.

I have learned even though I knew it before I went to Kashmir that in the Himalayas, the mountain vastness where there are temples, Buddhists, lamas, etc., that they are dead and decayed, that they have been vacant for many years. Those that are still open, the priest or the lama is out running for some public office and cannot be found. They are dirty, unkempt and the billions of dollars that were spent in the different parts of that part of the world building various monasteries of religions that have been dead for many years could have gone to help the people of that part of the world. There's been quite an influx of lamas in other teachings from that part of the world, yoga, Buddhist, etc. For instance, most recently in New York, there has been quite an influx of lamas from Tibet, Kashmir, Himalayas, etc. In a recent article, a fullpage spread of the *Daily News,* New York City, March 5th, the Sunday issue of 1978, the headline read "New York's Newest Gurus, Suddenly the Lamas of Tibet are all over town." It's almost as if the Pope had sent his top lieutenants to New York a mini-vatican. These lamas held meetings in New York Hilton's ballroom, packed. They have in their apartments a special room in which they hold meetings. They wear their robes; however, they sport the western style wristwatch, black horn-rimmed glasses which both are status symbols among their people.

I'm not saying that the Buddhists or those lamas aren't doing some good. It is a step for that person that may need it, but it's a waste of time if we could only have the teachings of ECK made aware to those vast majority of people in that part of the world, New York and its surrounding area. What ECKANKAR has to offer the individual there'd be quite a change to take place in New York City and its surrounding area. For an inspiring look at the Far East, I recommend the book "A Gift From The Master" by Alan Hammond (Illuminated Way Press).

Chapter 25

PRESENTING ECK IN ITS SIMPLEST FORM

The ECK ITSELF is able to demonstrate that we need to balance three parts of man which are: Physical, Soul and Spirit. Saints, saviours and many mystic teachers have clearly done this down through history. Some priests from the Catholic church have witnessed the blessing of several heaps of barley grain which the Sisters drew from for three months without the supply showing any signs of diminishing. This sort of thing can go on and on. There are many documented versions of supplying the need when necessary, and only when necessary.

One must expect this principle of the divine power of ECK. It is not a question of expecting to have; that which we desire is already waiting. This is the operation of the power in ECK. God's abundance is hidden in the creative invisible substance of ECK which contains all things yet does not wait for us to prove what wonders it can perform for we already know. When we are afraid to expect too much we don't ask, so the creative substance is not shaped by our thoughts and we are unable to receive. We find all sorts of queer excuses, such as, God is angry with us, God favors some people and not others, or that the work we are doing is not important enough to warrant SUGMAD's help. These reasons are most illogical because if you look around you, you'll see that some very good causes rarely seem to get enough funds for support and many of them with very low ideals seem to prosper.

Seems if a man is rich in the consciousness, intellectual gain for his own sake, he is just as handicapped. If he is rich in consciousness of personal vanity, the same will happen with him. When the consciousness is not locked in the realization of the kingdom within as it is in the outer worlds, it becomes as hard to enter as it is for a donkey to go through the eye of a needle. This is why it has been stated that the rich man, as well as the one strong in intellectuality, finds it hard to enter into the kingdom of heaven. This has puzzled man throughout the ages ever since Jesus told the young man to sell his goods and follow him. Ever since that time most men who have been seeking God, who have been rich or had any degree of material things, always felt that they must give them up, sell them, get rid of them. This is not so. For one can be rich in consciousness as well as the money for its own sake, and seek the narrow door within itself with the guidance of the Living ECK Master, which will lead to spiritual realization and spiritual greatness. However, if he is locked into the commercial bondage, he cannot enter into the true kingdom of God. There are three paths: the physical, emotional and the narrow way.

Those that mentalize and have difficulty getting beyond the mind, I say to you confidentially, in all sincerity there should be a profound humility in Soul at all times. When he is asking for that divine revelation to come to him, humility is that great step on the secret path of ECK and it will also be the last when conquered, when you reach this form of humility and retain it. Before the Divine ECK can begin to teach one through ITS own self-revelation, he must first become receptive, i.e., humble.

Intellectual ability and learning are admirable things and adorn a man, but intellectual pride puts a strong barrier between him and the Inner Master, which is ever calling to him and nudging silently.

The intellectual ones put themselves upon their pedestal and wait to be worshipped when all the while the Inner Master indwelling in the depths of their hearts is alone worthy to receive the recognition. The intellectual self seeks to strut like a proud peacock before the admiring gaze of the world. But the true begetter of his talents, and the creator of our achievements, the one who permeates it with the principle of life and thus permits it to exist, is quite content to remain in the background, unknown and unnoticed by man.

The intellectual purist will never be able to advance on the path of ECKANKAR. He is so busy trying to find mistakes and errors in the sacred writings of ECK that he overlooks what is necessary for his spiritual growth and defeats himself. This type of individual will rely on another ECKist and ask him to go to the inner planes to seek guidance for him. This is wrong for one must do this for his own self and not others.

It is one of the hardest tasks to abase oneself to the realization of one's own littleness, ignorance and vanity, yet it is the greatest of attainment for it leads directly to finding the divine life in its simplicity, which is the ECK. Then one can tell the world as he meets it day to day, for all who would lose the personal life gains a greater way of life.

In ECK one does not need the knowledge and culture of a distinguished mind to understand and appreciate the teachings of ECK. The simple, untutored, the primitive, can as readily enter into them by an act of faith and by practicing the spiritual exercises and can more easily enter into the heart of the SUGMAD. This always troubled the intellect of man.

As the thought, so the speech which is the chief revelation of the mind as a vehicle for the ECK. To present the message of ECK in the way of simplicity, you must be aware of each thought that is impressed upon your lips. Let the word of ECK be as genuine as the thought, as artless, as valid: think righteously, justly and speak frankly without the emotions as an evangelist or preacher trying to save Souls.

The great work for each Soul in ECK, is to lift the personal viewpoint out of the dual worlds of Kal into the pure positive God Worlds in consciousness that it becomes one with the whole, for only the humble can perceive the truth.

Paul Twitchell spoke of the existence of this ability, and the higher planes when he said to me, "I have much to say to you, but you cannot accept it all now. When the ECK enters into you IT shall lead you to truth." This points out that all can find the gift of Spirit within himself by effort, persistence and self-discipline.

Chapter 26

USE YOUR COMMON SENSE

By the time one reaches the fourth initiation in
ECKANKAR one should be so devoted to the
Living ECK Master in Spirit that he is a part of him.
It's a step that carries him up the ladder of God to
the lap of the Supreme Deity. This devotion is one in
which there is not one moment in wavering of love of
the Living ECK Master.

Very few people are capable of controlling the
emotions without having to think of being in the
higher states. For the very reason that emotions are
hard to control does one look in the direction of what
lies beyond; for after all, the emotional state is really
connected with the astral plane, although it is
believed to be an aspect of the highest reality of God
by some religious thought.

The immature individual, like the child, is usually
the result of his inability to control his environment.
When parents cannot cope with their own problems,
they are caught in a morass of their own emotional
disturbances and cannot give their children love and
affection or the understanding they need.
Consequently one part of the child's personality
becomes stifled. This shows in the adult who has
grown up under such circumstances, and those who
come to the Living ECK Master are greatly in need
of understanding love. Emotional disturbances
often find a symbolic outlet in the stomach or
intestinal system.

There is a code of ethics that a good number of
Higher Initiates as well as others have not applied;
this goes for all on this path of ECK as well as those

133

working in and for the ECK. Anyone having received the second initiation or greater and are still talking negatively, writing or criticizing other ECKists or the Living ECK Master carelessly and without thinking, will pay for the deed for it is a law not made by man.

"So many have the misconception that moral goodness is a requirement for spiritual salvation. This is not true. Moral goodness comes *only* from spiritual salvation." This statement, quoted from *The Spiritual Notebook*, pg. 170 by Sri Paul Twitchell, is often misunderstood.

When the individual has never had any self-discipline drilled into him and he becomes the victim of the Kal power, it is difficult for him to resist this negative power, but he must learn through self-discipline not to be used as a channel for Kal. He must know right from wrong, that is, the difference between the ECK and Kal power, so that he can permit the former to use him for his own benefit so that the universal worlds can be served while at the same time he is serving himself.

To use sex indiscriminately, to leave one mate to marry another or to go from one to another, thinking one has spiritual freedom, often is only to become involved in another state of affairs better known as negative karma. Therefore, one has not gained much spiritual freedom by the exchange of mates. The same applies when one leaves one religion to join another and usually learns that he has less freedom than previously. The mere changing of positions, locale and relationships does not necessarily mean that the individual is going to have peace, happiness or security in his life. This never comes in the changing of status in this world of human consciousness; for no peace, joy or security is found in wealth and health. Only the realization of God can release one from the fear of circumstances or conditions.

The Teacher is not interested in any outward manifestations for the chela, but desires to give help by gently probing and prying so the coiled springs of disturbed emotions within the chela can be loosened and brought into some positive action with love. It is this lack of love in the beginning, that creates the inability for correct guidance and actions of anyone. Man must love something; his work, family, neighbors, humanity or God, in order to have good spiritual survival. Attention focused upon any part of one's lower self leads to the vicious cycle of shyness, self-indulgence, and anti-social tendencies.

If sex is used for its legitimate purpose it becomes a high expression of love; otherwise, it falls into the trap of degradation which is one of those set up by the Kal power to keep Soul in this world. When one falls into the trap of self-indulgence, he begins to descend toward the animal plane. Nature has furnished man and woman with the proper means of perpetuating life on this planet. It is within the human species to decide what is best for themselves on the sex level; however, if they follow out the divine law that sex is not to become an instrument for self-indulgence, then all will be well. If sex is used lustfully, man simply wastes energy and clouds his mind, ending at last in blank stupidity like an ordinary animal. When sex controls the individual instead of him controlling it, the degeneration of that individual is already an established fact.

Ethics is a means of mind cleansing; although not a perfect means, at best it does prepare one to start on the path of God-Realization. When one reaches God-Realization, he becomes a spiritual traveler, is united with the Sound Current and with it, becomes a self-religious person. The Law of Karma is the underlying principle of personal responsibility. This is the law that brings back upon the doer, in spite of himself, the legitimate results of his own conduct. He must gather the fruits of his own reactions. Every action performed has its double karma, based upon this law. It affects the recipient and it returns upon the doer. This is the basis of ethics. It is a silent worker in the empire of man and matter, but in the higher universes where Spirit governs all, there is no karma because the higher law of wisdom, power and freedom supercedes all other laws.

Genuine ethics is the fruit of the trinity, wisdom, power and freedom, and this is the life-giving fruit of the great Sound Current. Once the individual understands that he is depending upon worldly goods, circumstances and human love to sustain him, he ceases to be his own worst enemy. He comes to that point where he is in love with all life, but his greatest affection is for God. He does not scatter his love among people openly but meets life in a manner of holding goodwill for all. His problem with the Kal power fades away and he becomes a shining example for many.

Sri Paul Twitchell told a small group of young people (and a few older people as well) at the Chicago Youth Conference in 1971 that the girls should retain their virginity until marriage and he stressed the same for the young men. Because a few have loose morals there are some religious groups out here on the West Coast telling others that those in ECKANKAR have no morals. This is an individual discipline and has nothing to do with ECKANKAR or Its teachings.

An article written in *The Oakland Tribune* by John Godwin, August 1972, about Sri Paul Twitchell stated: "He (Paul) blames moral laxity for most revolutions since the time of ancient Egypt and added the warning that there are forces now trying to build the same looseness of morals in our society here that will bring about the same results."

Chapter 27

SPIRITUAL DANGER OF DRUGS

There are entities who choose to serve the negative forces that dominate this world and they can influence or possess those who are strong-willed or who open their consciousness to psychic and occult experiences without proper protection.

Many young people have strange experiences when drugs are induced as an artificial means of leaving the physical body. This allows possession by negative or earthbound entities. It is very difficult to regain control of the physical vehicle after such an experience. It creates an imbalance, for some at once, others it may take weeks, months or several years.

The mind is a tool to be utilized for communications between Soul and the physical body. Since the mind is very impressionable, it is important that we use discrimination as to what we allow to become part of our consciousness.

Nothing is more depressing than to see the misguided using drugs to reach higher states of awareness. These people claim to have had a God-Realized experience, but nothing could be further from the truth. What the user does not understand is that he has deceived himself and has had only a small experience in the astral worlds beyond this physical plane. He has become a victim to that destructive mental action, lust. If allowed, lust develops into an abnormal demand of becoming destructive and degrading. The chief function of lust is to pull the user of drugs down to the common level of animals and keep him there.

Spiritual experiences are a reality and imagination is merely imagination. It is equally difficult to separate hallucination from spiritual experience, and thus mind-altering drugs are severely frowned upon in ECKANKAR and the danger of drugs to some neurotics is acknowledged.

Smoking marijuana pokes holes in individuals' auras just as certain negative aspects with drugs do. Think of the aura thus: you take a boat that is on the water, punch a hole in it and water comes in. If you think about the negative current doing damage to that vehicle, it is the same thing. We are involved in similar electromagnetic fields. The outer body is what is known as the astral sheath, and there is one on the causal and mental planes. Now each one of these is at a different rate of vibration, but the outermost is that known as the astral, the emotional part of man, and if a person is on drugs and opens this up to a spot in that aura, other negative things can flow through.

Once there is a puncture, that individual can clear it up himself with the spiritual exercises of ECKANKAR. No one else can do that for him. It is known as karma. It includes all abnormal desires, such as drugs, alcoholic drinks, tobacco and exotic foods which are eaten for the sake of enjoying the taste. This is why anyone approaching the teachings of ECK or an ECK Master to talk of drugs, as other artificial means for expanding the consciousness, is discouraged or turned away. The Supreme Deity will visit ITS glories upon Soul only when the latter has been prepared the natural way.

As the spiritual leader of ECKANKAR with thousands of followers around the world, I have seen devastating effects and have often been called upon to give spiritual assistance to those who have opened themselves to negative, psychic influences of marijuana. Drugs destroy the user's spiritual and physical ability to function as a truly complete human being.

Should the use of marijuana be legalized, this country and the world as a whole would become passive and weakened. This is especially dangerous because the user does not see that he has been deceived. Marijuana is a misdemeanor-type drug that is more than a misdemeanor in its effects.

Chapter 28

ECK AND REALITY IN ONE'S LIFE

Each year I receive thousands of letters, and personal requests for Akashic readings. I also get a number of requests and letters that pass over my desk from those who request an audience with Rebazar Tarzs and other ECK Masters. The people who write these letters do not understand that most of these great Souls have succeeded in their spiritual missions here, and have left the physical worlds, in a sense, and become mighty beings. One cannot have a physical audience with them, with any of them, but can see, talk and be advised by any, provided he is able to see them with spiritual eyes. However, there are those as Rebazar Tarzs, Fubbi Quantz and others who have survived hundreds of years on earth.

Up to this point, a chela has dealt mostly with dreams, images and mirages; however, at this point we must enter into the absolute truth. The teachings of the religionists have their followers believe in dead images—those which have been, but are no longer. In other words, what we usually see are the images of dead things which cannot help us in our spiritual growth here and now.

These are called "dead" because they are images of the past. An example: a strife between several countries, as in the East, because of religious conflicts between Moslems and Christians. Only spotlighting our attention on them gives them life. This is the dead image; the events that are made by the karma of today, and of the future; the part of our lives that comes out of the past into the present, and shapes our lives today.

I hope you understand an Akashic reading is scarcely more than a scanning of dead images to find something that has already existed, and perhaps made our lives what they are today. This is something few, if any, spiritual seekers want for themselves. What they are interested in is the live image.

Then, what is the live image? It is the image that the chela sees beyond the physical senses. It is not a vision, nor something conjured up in the imagination, but it is seeing reality for what it is with the spiritual eyes. It is not seeing into the future, nor looking into the past, but it is seeing and knowing the forces and currents that are always swirling around one. To know and understand these currents, and to see clearly the pictures of the spiritual world, is to have reality in one's life.

An ECKist learns rapidly that theories and doctrines of all kinds are the fabrications of the mind. We must be careful of this fabricating ability, for the resultant theories are misleading and can take us in the opposite direction of the God realm.

The pure image is very clear. It is reality of itself, and in it the ECKist will have varied experiences that do not come with false imagery. In the pure image one is able to see, know, have all the perceptions of color, smell, taste, hearing and feeling. This all comes through the spiritual eyes.

Most recently, a very learned man, an intellectual who was a professor in one of this country's universities, stepped aside from the Path of ECK. He doubted the works. He doubted the function of the Living ECK Master, and tried to dissect the teachings, tried to put it under a microscope, so to speak, as well as compare it to all other teachings that exist here on Earth. To do this, one is only bringing woe unto oneself, for to step upon the path for one's own selfishness is not being discriminatory.

The ECKist eventually arrives at the conclusion that faith is the only key to all his endeavors. In fact, he will go beyond the mere state of faith and enter into a knowingness that is far beyond the act of faith. While faith is important, it is not the actual fundamental principle of what we desire. The end result is knowingness. If he does not have this principle well established within himself, then the greater struggle to gain the abstract known as God will go on within himself until he has used every known mental and human device to gain a niche for himself in the ultimate reality.

When the seeker has reached the conclusion that whatever is his goal in the spiritual worlds cannot be reached by manipulating the mental processes, he will come to a pause in the struggle. There will be three roads at this junction: the left-hand road, which would lead to the physical path; the right-hand road to the mental worlds; and the road which leads straight ahead, and takes him into the spiritual realm. Most likely he would take the right-hand road, because most of his life it has been taught to him that this road leads into the spiritual realm, via the mental processes.

When man learns that the mental processes are stepping stones into the spiritual realm, then his whole life changes into a knowingness, belief and faith then are secondary causes; and unless he has the understanding and knowingness, all will be so many words, devices, techniques, and talk. He must reach this level via the road at the beginning, which is doubt.

We must either accept or deny the imagery that takes place within our own world. If we are perceptive enough, we can grasp that this imagery is outside of our own world, in what is called the universal worlds. The difference here is between the personal universe and the cosmic universe. But once this is understood, we can find the differences between the two and save ourselves a terrible amount of trouble.

I find that this is the downfall of those psychics who predict earthquakes, wars and other disasters that affect mankind. Unknowingly, they fall under the illusion of seeing a crackup in their own universe and mistake this for a universal disaster for they do not understand ECK-Vidya. They create panic among those who are gullible enough to believe such prophecies. The whole problem, though, is that the crackup in their own universe, which they witnessed, could be an indication of the splitting of their own personality, which leads to serious mental conditions.

The facts of pure imagery, or what we call reality, must become as acceptable to us as the facts of the physical senses. Therefore, no chela on the Path of ECK should allow himself to fall into the lower state. If he does, his work must be done all over again. He must know and understand that the basis of spiritual law is that when one is dwelling in the higher worlds, he is a law unto himself, because pure imagery is his experience. He is welcome to accept or reject it. This is the crux of the spiritual life. We become the law of ourselves and therefore must make our own decisions, have faith in what we experience and know that this is right. Until we accept this basic fact of ECKANKAR, we will not succeed in life in any manner whatsoever.

144

Chapter 29

DOUBT, A FACTOR IN
ONE'S SPIRITUAL GROWTH

Doubt of itself is a negative aspect of faith; however, if one looks at and investigates deeply, the spiritual works are rejected and without apparently no reason. It is found that the skeptical person will examine the spiritual works of ECK more thoroughly than others before entering into it. He is better prepared than those who plunge deeply or blindly into ECK without thinking or finding reasons in his actions hoping it will resolve some personal problem or give the individual instant success in God-Realization. The individuals of this type are actually a detriment to the ECK Master for he must work mostly with the people who make good use of their discriminatory faculties.

With the development of one's discrimination faculty, honing it to a fine point, he is at the mercy of the mind which can run wild and land in some sort of trouble. This is where doubt is used as a restraint and not at all negative as so many people believe. If one doubts the works of ECK in the beginning, it means that if he studies and examines it at any length, he is apt to become a greater chela than those who fall into it from the very start, hoping to use it for their own salvation. None can do themselves a greater service than this.

This brings me to the heart of my subject which are the classes in ECK. We have a great number of Satsang classes and there will be more. As we grow spiritually at the steady slow pace we've been growing, we must have a foundation under ourselves individually to be prepared for what lies ahead on our journey to the God-conscious experience and total awareness.

There are tools in *Letters to Gail* that assist the individual to fend for himself, to think for himself and to ward off any psychic enemies for himself. If you really want to help the Living ECK Master, first make the preparation for the foundation with the study of several introductory books, then the ECK Satsang and individual ECK discourses to build the foundation.

A letter came across my desk recently from an Initiate and he had this to say: "I have read *Letters to Gail* all the way through before and I recently reread the book at the rate of two to three letters per day. It helped to keep a good continuity and see the letters as connected. The information kept building and I could see how each step helped make more sense in the following letters, etc. Before, I would just pick up the book and read a letter here or there and it wasn't as good." And this is true.

Take the individual who speed-reads and goes back through it later at a slower pace or takes it letter by letter or two or three letters at a time and discusses it with others, he'll get more out of it. In working spiritually with those who haven't grasped the ECK teachings, I am having to go back with some people and make sure that they have that foundation or the preparation for a foundation. You'll find many things fall into place by taking the *Letters to Gail* and read two or three letters (no more than three I'd say) at one sitting, once a day. It doesn't matter but go slow. Don't try to memorize that which you come across or what may be the underlying meaning of it, but you'll find that the written word of ECK cannot be read at a rapid pace to get much out of it, or to absorb that which ECK is able to give you.

This individual's letter went on to say, "The book helped a great deal in learning some practical ways of staying up at the survival level above the lower planes. It is a special feeling of detachment that I can't describe very easily, at least not very briefly. It also is very encouraging to me in believing more and more in myself and that I can take charge of my thoughts and emotions and manage them in the best interests of myself and others."

There are many individuals that reach a state of doubt and this is the opposite of knowing and does bring him to a state of qualms. But if he is honest with himself and he knows that this is only a level of consciousness in which he is presently engaged, the prime requirement of the path of ECK is honesty. One may fool himself but not the elemental laws of ECK. So the Initiate's real struggle on the path will be with his own state of consciousness and not with the spiritual law itself, nor with any elements of ECK. He will soon learn that the Inner Master through the ECK will develop within him a persistance which defeats anything that is in opposition to the purpose of ECK of Itself.

With that in mind we become aware of the exacting Law of ECK, i.e., that Spirit triumphs, ECK rules and the ECK commands. This makes the ECK the greatest spiritual force of all ages and the universal spiritual works. Sri Paul Twitchell has written about this in various publications as I have read it from *The Shariyat-Ki-Sugmad* at the various Golden Wisdom Temples. He who doubts this in the beginning will learn in time that nothing triumphs in life unless it has the element of ECK in its own nature. What is happening here is that we are entering into the self-knowledge state, and self-knowledge is therefore a slow, painful stage and we must look at ourselves objectively and say, "What do I really want of life? What is it that I really need? Is this the real path of God."

When the individual gets tired of mentalizing which is a doubtful stage of wasting time and intellectualizing about people and things, or about the Living ECK Master and the works of ECK, he gets off the doubtful stage into the spiritual arena. He learns to weed out things, learns to release this mental garbage. It is like buying a pair of new shoes for we must learn to release the old ones in order to make way for the new. If someone becomes a problem, we must not feel guilty but release that individual. This brings about emotional and spiritual release of life. It gives us the strength to be ourselves. Yet those close to us may not understand. If we cannot make ourselves happy, then we cannot make others happy.

One must come to the understanding that the followers of ECK must cultivate the very virtues which make us unconquerable by those in the lower worlds. With that in mind, then the individual should be able to see that ECK is the rallying point against the works of Kal and its negative powers. To do what we should do in the name of God is the whole law of the consciousness for it takes us into the very heart of God. It does away with doubt and leaves no guess work. It brings a knowingness that we must always be the foundation of the spiritual life of ECK, in the preparation for the foundation and the building blocks the individual will find in *Letters to Gail,* which will prepare one for greater works to enrich the consciousness and allow it to expand beyond the mind. Then the individual will be able to live and move in the SUGMAD.

Chapter 30

THE ECK MOVEMENT

ECKANKAR was brought to the masses in 1965 by Sri Paul Twitchell, a soft-spoken Southern gentleman of small stature, penetrating blue eyes, with a wealth of spiritual experiences in the Far Country. Under the guidance of the ECK Master Rebazar Tarzs, who appeared to Paul nightly in the Soul body with instructions, Paul brought forth the age-old message of ECKANKAR through discourses and books, followed up by lectures and travels around the world.

I was very fortunate to travel with Paul often, becoming more aware of the responsibility he carried as the MAHANTA, the Living ECK Master, a responsibility I was to accept myself upon his translation (death) in 1971.

Many half-truths and untruths have been stated about the ECK movement by people who are uninformed about Its message and Its purpose. In this chapter, I wish to share some questions and answers that involve the ECKANKAR movement, in an effort to shed light upon a subject that has interested millions. The message of ECK can never be repeated too often, for as a Way of Life, a very Sacred Way of Life, it has proven to be a path millions have hungered for, for many lifetimes.

Some of these questions and answers have appeared in articles by Brad Steiger in *Sybil Leek's Journal* and a variety of tabloids and other publications.

WHAT IS ECKANKAR?

We are born alone and we die alone. Once an individual experiences ECKANKAR, he finds it very difficult to put into words. It is a way to God-Realization, and spells spiritual freedom. When man loosens and lets go, he finds himself guided to the liberation of Soul. From liberation comes total freedom, total awareness, and total responsibility—the keys to heaven. The fundamental teaching of ECK is that these attributes may be most readily achieved through travel in the Soul body.

CAN DRUGS ASSIST ONE IN THE STUDY OF ECKANKAR?

It is each man's responsibility to live in God-Realization as much as possible without losing any of its effect in his daily life; it is only reasonable that we should take the way that God has provided for us and not the way that man wants to take to get there faster by artificial agents. If man relies on such methods, all life becomes an illusion; he is in danger of forsaking his responsibility to life and becoming a burden to society.

WHAT ABOUT CERTAIN TECHNIQUES OF MEDITATION, MIGHT THEY BE HELPFUL IN ACHIEVING SPIRITUAL FREEDOM IN ECKANKAR?

ECKANKAR is active, not passive. We aren't concerned with sitting around contemplating our navels. We try never to make the error of confusing the microcosm with the macrocosm. In ECKANKAR, one works constantly toward developing complete spiritual freedom, total awareness, and total responsibility. The trouble with so many meditative techniques under the guidance of various masters is that they do not grant their chelas their freedom. They retain their hold on the individual.

When the student of ECKANKAR has completed his course of study, he is free to ask the Living ECK Master to accept the role as his Master or he is free to go on his way. It is not the way of ECKANKAR to demand a hold that lasts for the life of the student. It is the way of ECKANKAR to set the individual free to accept his own responsibility and to stand on his own feet. We definitely do not encourage anyone "dropping out" of society. In ECKANKAR, we seek to improve the social order, not to retreat from its problems and responsibilities.

HEAVEN HAS MORE THAN ONE PLANE OF EXISTENCE?

In ECKANKAR, we learn that the heavenly worlds are comprised of many planes of existence, each denoting a certain amount of spiritual growth and level of consciousness. Man does not need to die before he enters heaven. Death need not be man's only ticket to the heavenly worlds. He may, through the practice of the spiritual exercises of ECKANKAR, transcend his mantle of flesh and daily soar unencumbered through the mighty God Worlds.

The student of ECKANKAR can have the opportunity of visiting any plane he wishes, or the option of making trips to the various levels of existence at his own volition. It must be remembered, however, that Soul Travel is concerned mainly with movement of Soul in the lower worlds, that of the regions from the physical planes to the fifth plane, which is the first of these ethereal regions named as the worlds of pure Spirit. Once there, we are within the true kingdom and no longer need movement or travel. Soul is beyond time and space, which is existent within the lower planes, the physical, astral, causal, mental, and etheric planes.

Those who have Soul travelled include Sudar Singh of India, the Sufi Saints Guru Nanak, Jalaldin'l Rumi, Shamus-i-Tabriz, St. Anthony of Padua, Padre Pio, Omar Khayyam, St. Bernard, Capuchin, Kabir, Zoroaster, Firdusi, St. Paul, Jesus, Buddha, Tulsi Das, Jack London, L. Adam Beck, Harriet

Beecher Stowe, Elizabeth Barrett Browning, Lord Byron, Shelley, Marie Corelli, George DuMaurier, Balzac, St. John, the Apostle, who as Prestor John, lived to be 1,000 years old.

Many spiritual teachers, saviors and mystics have tried to tell man to separate Soul from body. As long as Soul stays within these five planes which constitute the psychic worlds, it is dealing with time and space, and therefore with movement or travel. As soon as Soul reaches the upper planes of God, the concepts of time and space are meaningless. Soul is in a state of total awareness and travel becomes unnecessary. Soul is in a state of God-Realization, absolute consciousness. It is the achievement of this state that ECKANKAR is all about.

DOES ECK BELIEVE THAT ONE MAY ACQUIRE SPIRITUAL GUIDES?

Not if you mean that in the old spiritualist sense. ECKANKAR does teach that there exists a vast spiritual hierarchy operating throughout all the universes. This hierarchy is very important to the chelas of ECK, for the Beings who comprise this hierarchy play a key role in each student's development. An earnest chela will be taken nightly from his physical body to travel to other planes. There he will be given instruction by an ECK Master.

The chela will first meet his Master in the Light Worlds, where the Master will be waiting to linkup his light body with that of the chela. Then the Master will take him to one of the seven Golden Wisdom Temples to study.

CAN'T ONE TRAVEL ON THESE PLANES ON HIS OWN, WITHOUT AN ECK MASTER?

Yes, but even in spontaneous out-of-body experiences, the Soul's progress is always watched so It does not encounter any psychic snarls on the way. The great advantage in traveling with the ECK

Master, of course, is that he will make suggestion
and steer you in certain directions in order that you
gain the greatest benefit from your journey.

ISN'T THERE A DANGER THAT SOME
ADEPTS MAY CONSIDER THEMSELVES AS
REMOVED FROM THE WORLD AND MAY
SEEK TO DROP THEIR RESPONSIBILITIES?

No. While ECKANKAR teaches its followers to
remain detached from worldly concerns, it still
teaches its members to fulfill their social and family
obligations. ECKANKAR, properly practiced, can
never be used as an excuse to keep from discharging
a duty, or to keep from interacting responsibly with
the world. The trick is in detachment. One must love
his family, do his daily labor, fulfill his role as a
citizen, without becoming bound to any of them.
Unless we are heading for the ultimate goal of Soul-
awareness within the realm of God, we should
examine our values in life.

IS THE STUDY OF ECKANKAR MADE UP
LARGELY OF SECRET DOCTRINES AND
ANCIENT FORMULAS?

The knowledge to be gained from a study of
ECKANKAR is not hidden, nor can any of it be dis-
tilled into pat formulas or something which can be
read from a book. The knowledge of ECKANKAR
lies in a process which the neophyte slowly develops
and prepares for himself. The chela does not acquire
the power, but rather, he becomes a part of it.
Neither does he accept the power; it accepts him.

The basic principle of ECKANKAR is that the
world of creation is finished and that the original of
all things lies within man. Therefore, the way by
which each person can regain the original mastership
of his own "Garden of Eden" is by use of the faculty
of imagination with which the SUGMAD (God) has
endowed each of us as his divine gift to all men.

ECKANKAR teaches that we can have comfort in the higher states of consciousness and in Soul Travel experiences, such as those which were common in the lives of the old Christian saints and the lives of the Eastern adepts.

All those who strive to attain perfection in this life will follow a path similar to the one which one follows in ECKANKAR. A teacher from the other worlds, or from this one, will appear at the time when the chela reaches a certain period of his spiritual life. The period of instruction may be difficult, but the end result is well worth the struggle.

WHY DOES ECKANKAR EMPHASIZE THE SOLACE AND COMFORT GAINED BY ITS TEACHINGS? WHY DO YOU INSIST THAT EXPERIENCES ARE SO IMPORTANT?

Well, let me put it this way. Man, being mortal, must one day leave his fleshly cloak; so it is important that he should learn by going in and out of the body that he can give up the material shell at the time of physical death without suffering and anxiety.

THE ECK MASTERS AND TEACHERS ARE BEINGS FROM THE SPIRITUAL HIERARCHY. CAN THEY BE COMPARED TO THE MORE COMMON CONCEPT OF SAINTS, WHO ACT AS INTERMEDIARIES BETWEEN GOD AND MAN?

These spiritual travelers refuse to consider themselves as intermediaries between the Supreme Being and man. Of course, they are the agents of the SUGMAD, God, but they will not allow any mortal to rely upon them as a support.

WHAT IS MEANT BY GOD-REALIZATION?

When the mind gives up its inner tensions, this experience of light and sound comes pouring into Soul like a violent flood. God-Realization may often be sudden, unexpected, and spontaneous. It lifts into the heights of the True Kingdom and snaps us out of the sleep state into the consciousness of awareness. In God-Realization we are now alive. The whole secret of our strength lies not in the fact that we have the secret of power, but of life itself.

HOW WOULD YOU DEFINE YOUR ROLE AS A TEACHER OF ECKANKAR?

First of all, in dealing with people, I seldom use the word chela, student. Once such roles as those of student and teacher are accepted by the seeker, he may persist in identifying himself as such. This is one of the lower aspects of all metaphysical teachings, for it raises one and puts another in a lower class.

Since we are all spiritually equal, no ECK Master is going to stress the fact that he is on a higher level than another, regardless of his place on the spiritual pathway. The Adepts of the Ancient Order of the Vairagi declare that each of us has esoteric knowledge within us and that in some, this knowledge is of a higher degree simply because they have come to recognize it a bit sooner than others.

IS ECKANKAR THE ONLY PATH TO GOD?

I am well aware that there are many approaches to God, for nobody has a monopoly on any path. God is, and, of course, Soul is, since Soul is a part of God. When we understand this as truth, then we learn that all a teacher can do is to put our feet upon a path and point the way. No one teacher, living or past, can give us the actual understanding of truth. The knowledge and understanding of truth is wholly dependent upon the individual to make his way to truth.

When one reaches a certainty of this spiritual knowledge, he suddenly knows the secret of the ages. He has learned the simplest of all things, that ach one of us is truth itself. We are the living truth, the very embodiment of God. The essential nature of ECKANKAR is freedom from all things—the complete independence of Soul.

COULD YOU TELL US EXACTLY WHAT THE ECK-VIDYA IS AND FROM WHAT TRADITION IT STEMS?

The ECK-Vidya is the Atma science of prophecy used mainly by the Adepts of the secret order of the Vairagi, the brotherhood of those great Masters who follow the path of ECKANKAR, the ancient science of Soul Travel. The ECK-Vidya is more inclusive than astrology or any of the mystical arts utilized by the ancient and modern prophets of psychic precognition. The art of the ECK-Vidya is only an aspect of ECKANKAR, which is the fulfillment of God-Realization. The ECK-Vidya has always been a part of the training for all ECK Masters. It has been handed down from one Master to another since the dawn of time, for there has always been a Living ECK Master here on earth to take care of those who follow the path of ECKANKAR.

Very few people today use this ancient method of prophecy, for the old instructions of divination, which were handed down by oral teachings, have gone underground. The Masters of ECKANKAR, who are able to use the ECK-Vidya techniques of checking a person's past, present, and future, have dwindled to a handful, headed mainly by Fubbi Quantz, the ECK Master who is the Abbot of the Katsupari Monastery near the old site of the Voice of Akisvasha, an oracle still active in the wild mountain ranges of northern Tibet near an unexplored site called Tirmer.

HOW WOULD YOU COMPARE THE ACCURACY OF THE ECK-VIDYA TO ASTROLOGY?

As I just stated, the two work in altoge different fields. Astrology is a mechanical f stating only the prospects of what could take pla while the ECK-Vidya is more accurate for it de nitely states the karmic pattern that shows the ind vidual having certain happenings and events in his life. The ECK-Vidya reader is above the planes of time and space and can see the past and future time track. He does not work with ESP, but with the definite reading of the record of the individual Soul.

The Soul embodiments of past lives are similar to tiny file cards; each is a life with a series of these pictures beginning at birth and passing through all events to death, on whatever plane It has embodied Itself. Looking further, the reader can see what is going to happen to the individual in the present life and future lives. Astrology cannot be read any further than a few years ahead in this life. Maybe through a whole life, but not into any future lives.

CAN ANYONE LEARN TO DO THE
ECK-VIDYA, OR DO YOU HAVE TO
BE AN ADEPT? CAN IT BE TAUGHT?

Those Initiates of the Fifth Circle in ECKANKAR can generally learn to do the ECK-Vidya. Naturally, only a few will attain this level, but the ECK-Vidya is one of the thirty-two aspects of which is developed in learning the spiritual works of ECK. Those few who have learned it are showing spiritual development, but then one day, they will cease to read publicly as I have, because of lack of time, or because they have risen above this stage of unfoldment in their advancing toward God-Realization. In some cases it is taught to the individual who has reached the state of the fifth initiation in ECK.

WHAT DO YOU MEAN WHEN YOU REFER
TO THE ZIQUIN OF THE ECK-VIDYA?

The ZIQUIN means above the psychic planes. ZI

word in the Amdo language, the dialect of a
community of persons on the border of northeast
Tibet and China. It is in this region that ECK has
been most prominent and most well known. ZI
means above, and the word QUIN is five; therefore,
ZIQUIN means above the fifth plane, the plane from
which the ECK-Vidya readings are made.

WHAT DOES THE ECK-VIDYA HAVE TO SAY
ABOUT REINCARNATION AND KARMA?

The ECK-Vidya works with the twin theory of
reincarnation and karma. It tries to explain and
show how each is integrated in the life of every
person. It also shows how karma may be worked out
in a single lifetime and that one does not have to
return to this world. That is, after the individual
becomes an Initiate of ECKANKAR.

INDEX

Suggested introductory books published by IWP on ECKANKAR, the most ancient spiritual teaching in all the universes . . .

IN MY SOUL, I AM FREE
(Biography on Sri Paul Twitchell by Brad Steiger)

YOUR RIGHT TO KNOW
(Compilation of articles on contemporary subjects)

THE TIGER'S FANG
(An understanding of levels of heaven)

THE FLUTE OF GOD (Psychology of Spirit)

THE SPIRITUAL NOTEBOOK
(History of ECKANKAR)

STRANGER BY THE RIVER
(Love and wisdom of the ages)

LETTERS TO GAIL, VOLS. I & II
(Basic text)

FROM HEAVEN TO THE PRAIRIE
(Biography of Sri Darwin Gross)

Books on ECKANKAR can be found or ordered at your local bookstore.

In many areas around the world, discussion classes on the introductory books of ECKANKAR are being held, which the public is welcome to attend. ECKANKAR Centers will be listed in the local telephone book. For more information on ECKANKAR and/or ECKANKAR activities, please write to:

ECKANKAR
P.O. Box 3100
Menlo Park, CA 94025-0600

For a free book catalog, write:

PUBLISHING
P.O. Box 2449
Menlo Park, CA 94025-0052 U.S.A.

BOOK ORDER COUPON

Mail to:

 PUBLISHING
P.O. Box 2449
Menlo Park, CA 94025-0052 U.S.A.

☐ Please send me a complete IWP catalog.

I enclose $_____ for the book(s) checked below.

Foreign countries: Please remit Int'l M.O. or
check payable in U.S. funds to IWP PUBLISHING.

0104	___ **In My Soul I Am Free** $2.95	$_____
0106	___ **The Tiger's Fang** $2.50 papbk	_____
0106S	___ **The Tiger's Fang** $8.95 hb	_____
0110	___ **Your Right to Know** $1.95 papbk	_____
011099	___ **Your Right to Know** $8.95 hb	_____
011299	___ **From Heaven to the Prairie** $14.95	_____
0126	___ **The Flute of God** $2.95	_____
0128	___ **The Spiritual Notebook** $2.50	_____
0132	___ **Stranger by the River** $5.95	_____
0154	___ **Letters to Gail, Vol. I** $5.95 papbk	_____
0155	___ **Letters to Gail, Vol. II** $9.95 hb	_____

Total $_____

6% sales tax (California only) $_____

Add 10% for shipping $_____
75¢ minimum

TOTAL ENCLOSED $_____

Name _____
(please print)

Street _____

City _____ State_____

Country _____ Postal Code_____

999903

□ I am interested in information on discussion or study groups in my area.

□ Please send me more information on ECKANKAR.

Mail to:

ECKANKAR
P.O. Box 3100
Menlo Park, CA 94025
U.S.A.

detach here

Name _____

Street _____

City_____ State _____

Country _____ Zip _____

9